Good luck!

LIVING WITH
ATAXIA

An information
and resource guide

Martha A. Nance, MD
for the
National Ataxia Foundation

National Ataxia Foundation
15500 Wayzata Boulevard, #750
Wayzata, Minnesota 55391

(612) 473-7666 Telephone
(612) 473-9289 Fax

ISBN: 0-943218-09-8

Library of Congress
Catalog Card Number: 96-72598

Edited by: Linda Hanner and Carol J. Frick
Illustrations: Linda Hanner
Book design: Carol J. Frick

Acknowledgments

I HAVE MANY people to thank for the creation of this book. First and foremost, the original inspiration for the book came from the Louisiana Chapter of the National Ataxia Foundation, and many of their original words have survived the various revisions of the text.

Arnie Gruetzmacher provided the information on financial planning. Parts of the section on medical management of ataxia were adapted from a talk called "Pills and Problems" given by Dr. Michael A. Wilensky on July 19, 1995.

The book would never have been completed without the editorial assistance of Linda Hanner and Carol J. Frick, who kept us on track and more or less on schedule. DeNiece Roach, president of the NAF board of directors, likewise, would never quite let me forget to complete the project.

I would not be a student of ataxia had I not had a teacher, Dr. Lawrence Schut (NAF Medical Director). He and Dr. S.H. Subramony (NAF Research Director) have contributed both directly and indirectly to this volume.

However, most of what I really know about ataxia I have learned from you. I won't name you all because the list would be too long and I might accidentally leave someone out, but you know who you are! Thank you all, and I hope this helps.

Martha A. Nance, MD
Medical Research Liaison
National Ataxia Foundation

Contents

Introduction

Having ataxia has changed the course of my life and has meant facing different kinds of challenges, but it certainly hasn't prevented me from enjoying life. Sometimes I feel my life is fuller than most other people's.
—Steve Huffer, Texas

AS HUMANS, we experience a variety of emotions in reaction to life's varied experiences—joy, sorrow, pleasure, pain, fear, contentment, anger, acceptance. A diagnosis of ataxia and the realization of its enormous impact on one's life is almost certain to bring with it some of the more unpleasant emotions, at least initially. The implications of a progressive disorder often seem overwhelming.

Ataxia almost invariably causes significant changes in the life course one has anticipated. However, as many with ataxia have testified, ataxia doesn't change the fact that one is human. And it doesn't preclude one from experiencing the more pleasurable human emotions—or from living a rewarding, productive life.

Steve Huffer was just 15 years old when he was diagnosed as having a hereditary form of ataxia, but he has gone on to live a full life. After high school, he attended and graduated from college and has worked full time as a computer programmer. At 34, he says he also leads an active social life and loves to travel. Steve is just one of many with ataxia who feel they have rewarding lives.

With or without ataxia, we all have good and bad

experiences, joys and disappointments. The diagnosis of ataxia will most likely mean letting go of some prior goals and dreams. It might no longer be feasible to be captain of the football team or climb a mountain, but one can set new aspirations. People with ataxia can still be loving parents and friends, and active, contributing community members.

This book is written to help you understand what ataxia is and how it can affect a person physically and emotionally. We hope the information and insights will help you to adjust and to live a gratifying life.

Many of the people who have contributed to this book have shared the journey with you. They have ataxia, or they have cared for family members with ataxia, or they are health professionals who have worked with people who have ataxia.

In recent years, scientists have made great strides in unraveling the mysteries of ataxia, and the work to find better treatments continues. But until there is no more ataxia, it is up to all of us to find ways to improve our lives and the lives of others who have ataxia.

Understanding ataxia

What is ataxia?

What does genetics have to do with it?

What is ATAXIA?

Ataxia (the symptom) and ATAXIA (the disease)

Ataxia comes from a Greek word meaning "without order." The word today means the same thing as "incoordination."

Ataxia can be a symptom of many disorders, including those associated with certain toxins, infections, and degenerative changes in the nervous system. The word "ataxia" might simply be used to mean poor coordination, or it might be used in a more specific way to denote a degenerative disease of the nervous system. In this section, we will use ataxia to mean the symptom of incoordination, and ATAXIA, in small capital letters, to refer to one of the degenerative diseases that cause ataxia.

Some types of ATAXIA are "hereditary," which means they run in families, and some types don't appear to have any hereditary connection. Sometimes one kind of ATAXIA can be distinguished from another by the symptoms. All forms of ATAXIA cause ataxia (poor coordination). Some forms also cause additional symptoms that make them easier to distinguish from one another. Often, particularly if the symptoms are mild, a physician can't be certain which type of ATAXIA the patient has.

Hereditary ataxia refers to a group of inherited diseases which have in common that they cause degeneration of the *cerebellum* or its pathways.

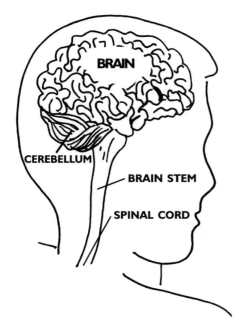

BRAIN

CEREBELLUM

BRAIN STEM

SPINAL CORD

The cerebellum is the "coordination center" of the brain, so any disease that affects the cerebellum can cause loss of coordination. Coordination is particularly important for walking, performing complex movements of the fingers and hands, moving the tongue and lips to speak and swallow, and for smooth movements of the eyes. Thus, individuals with disorders affecting the cerebellum often notice poor balance when walking, inability to run, clumsiness of the hands, a change in speech, or abnormal eye movement.

Breakthroughs in understanding ATAXIA

In the 1980s, new methods for imaging the brain were developed to help detemine the location and nature of brain and nervous system disorders. Computerized tomography (CT) and, more important, magnetic resonance imaging (MRI) can show whether the cerebellum or nearby parts of the brain or spinal cord have been affected by a stroke, tumor, infection, or degenerative disease.

The greatest breakthroughs in ATAXIA research in the 1990s have been the discovery of several genes that cause ATAXIA. Genetic tests and refined brain imaging techniques allow physicians to make more accurate and specific diagnoses in individuals with ataxia than was possible in the past.

Sporadic adult-onset ataxia

Perhaps the largest group of individuals with ataxia are those whose symptoms begin in adulthood and who are unaware of any other similarly affected individuals in their family. This is called *sporadic ataxia.*

These patients are the most difficult for physicians to diagnose correctly because there are any number of acquired and hereditary causes of ataxia which must be ruled out before a diagnosis of sporadic ataxia can be made with any confidence, and there is no test that can confirm the diagnosis accurately.

The symptoms of sporadic adult-onset ataxia are variable, but may take one of two general forms:

▶ The symptoms are isolated to the cerebellum and primarily cause incoordination. In this case the disability may progress slowly and be compatible with long survival. This can be called *pure cerebellar degeneration,* meaning that other parts of the brain are not involved.

▶ Ataxia is accompanied by additional symptoms such as neuropathy (any dysfunctions of the nerves), dementia (impaired intellectual function), or weakness, rigidity or spasticity of the muscles. In this case the disability may be greater and progress more quickly. This can be called *sporadic olivopontocerebellar ataxia,* or *sporadic OPCA.*

It is important to understand that the diagnosis of sporadic ataxia cannot be arrived at quickly or simply by an office examination. Depending on the situation, the physician may need to rule out other causes of ataxia, such as stroke, a brain tumor or cancer elsewhere in the body, congenital malformations of the brain, vitamin deficiencies, or exposures to certain toxins. If there is a significant history of alcohol use or abuse, it may be impossible to determine whether the ataxia is due to the toxic effects of alcohol on the cerebellum or peripheral nerves or to other disorders. Thus, a patient whose final diagnosis is sporadic ataxia should expect to have had a number of blood tests, CT or MRI of the brain or spinal cord, or electromyography (EMG) before being told of the diagnosis.

Another area of difficulty for patients with sporadic ataxia and their physicians is what to tell the relatives. It might be impossible to say whether a person with sporadic ataxia has a hereditary disease which was simply not diagnosed in other family members, or has a condition caused by unknown factors in the environment.

Factors that can make the diagnosis of a hereditary disease difficult include early death of key individuals, or estrangement or lack of communication between relatives due to adoption or other reasons. Occasionally, a hereditary disease occurs for the first time in a family because of a new change or mutation in a gene.

Hereditary adult-onset ataxias

▶ **SCA1** *Spinocerebellar ataxia type 1* is also called Schut's disease, hereditary olivopontocerebellar atrophy (OPCA), or Marie's ataxia. Research in SCA1 began in the 1940s, led by two U.S. neurologists whose families were at risk for developing

SCA1. Success in SCA1 research came in 1993 when researchers in Minnesota and Texas identified the responsible gene. Finding the SCA1 gene was only the beginning for researchers, who are still working to understand the disease well enough to find an effective treatment or cure for it. But finding the gene was important, because now for the first time there is a simple blood test that can accurately diagnose this kind of ataxia.

The onset of symptoms in SCA1 is usually in adulthood, with the average age being in the mid-30s. The first symptom is usually incoordination of the hands and trouble with balance when walking. Difficulty swallowing and indistinct speech are common as SCA1 progresses over a period of several years. Some individuals develop additional symptoms such as neuropathy (loss of feeling and reflexes in the feet or legs), spasticity, weakness, or memory troubles, but these are not present in all people with SCA1. When the onset of symptoms is at a younger age (before age 20), symptoms in addition to ataxia occur more frequently.

The duration of symptoms in SCA1 varies from one person to another, and seems to vary a little from one family to another. However, the disease is always measured in years, not weeks or months.

SCA1 is an *autosomal dominant disease* (see glossary or the chapter on genetics). This term means that individuals of either sex are equally likely to inherit the gene and develop the disease, and that it passes directly from one generation to the next without skipping generations. Anyone who has SCA1 should know that each of his or her children has a 50 percent chance of inheriting the SCA1 gene. Although only a neurologic examination can determine whether a person has symptoms of SCA1, the presence of the gene can accurately be detected by a blood test.

▶ **SCA2** *Spinocerebellar ataxia type 2* (chromosome 12-linked ataxia) is an autosomal dominant, adult-onset form of ataxia which has symptoms very similar to SCA1 and SCA3. People with SCA2 often have neuropathy and very slow eye movements in addition to ataxia. Muscle cramps and tremor are early symptoms in some patients. The gene was identified by researchers in California, France, and Japan in 1996. At the time this manual was written, gene testing for this disorder was not yet available clinically.

▶ **MJD** *Machado-Joseph disease* (also called SCA3) is another autosomal dominant form of hereditary ataxia. The name Machado-Joseph combines the family names of the first two families described with the condition (in 1972). Both families had their origins in the Portugese Azore Islands. At one time MJD was thought to be a very rare disease found only in certain isolated ethnic groups. But gene research has now shown that MJD is in fact much more common than SCA1. The gene responsible for MJD was identified by a team of researchers from Japan in 1993. Like SCA1, a blood test can now accurately diagnose the presence or absence of the gene change that causes MJD.

The symptoms of MJD may be more wide-ranging than those of SCA1. Like SCA1, the disease usually begins in mid-adult life and progresses over a number of years (an average of 15 years in one study, with some patients surviving for almost 30 years after the onset of symptoms). Onset in adolescence or as late as age 70 has been seen. As for all forms of ataxia, the first symptom is usually impaired balance, followed later by incoordination of the hands or slurring of the speech. Some individuals notice double vision. To the physician, limitation of eye movements, abnormally slow eye movements, or a "staring" appearance of the eyes may be a clue that the disease is MJD.

As MJD progresses, additional neurologic symptoms such as spasticity, rigidity, loss of muscle bulk and strength, and slowness of movement are common. Although there is no treatment for the underlying disease, symptoms such as fatigue, depression, sleep disturbance, pain, or tremor, which develop in some affected individuals, may improve with medications. For this reason, if you have MJD, it is important to report to your doctor any symptoms that bother you.

▶ **SCA4** *Spinocerebellar ataxia type 4* has been reported in one family. It is an autosomal dominant, adult-onset form of ataxia in which ataxia, stiffness or slowness of movements, and neuropathy involving mostly the sensory nerves are the most prominent symptoms. The eye movements are reported to be normal. The gene has not been identified yet, so gene testing is not possible, but it is known to be located on chromosome 16.

▶ **SCA5** *Spinocerebellar ataxia type 5* is sometimes called "Holmes ataxia" after Dr. Gordon Holmes, who first described the condition in 1907, or "Lincoln's ataxia" because one family with the condition is related to President Abraham Lincoln. SCA5 is an autosomal dominant form of ataxia. Its effects appear to be much more limited to the cerebellum than the other dominant ataxias. The gene or genes responsible for SCA5 have not been identified yet, but one responsible gene has been localized to chromosome 11.

The onset of symptoms may be later in SCA5 than for the other ataxias described above, often later than age 50. Because the effects are largely limited to the cerebellum, individuals affected with SCA5 may live for decades after their symptoms begin. Symptoms of SCA5 are generally restricted to impaired coordination of the hands, arms, and legs, impairment of balance in walking, and indistinct, dysarthric (unclear) speech. Walking difficulties may progress to the point that a wheelchair provides a sensible aid to mobility. Since thinking, swallowing, bowel and bladder control, and strength are usually not affected, people with SCA5 usually continue to live independently.

▶ **SCA7** *Spinocerebellar ataxia type 7* has also been called autosomal dominant cerebellar ataxia type 2, or ataxia with pigmentary retinopathy. This is an autosomal dominant form of ataxia in which the earliest symptoms often have to do with vision. Affected individuals notice changes in visual acuity and color vision. These changes may progress until the person is legally blind. In addition, symptoms of ataxia, slow eye movements, and mild changes in sensation or reflexes may be detectable. Symptoms seem to begin a little earlier in this condition than in some of the other adult-onset ataxias, with the average onset being in the mid-20s. Sometimes the onset of symptoms is in childhood (onset as early as age four has been reported). Early identification of this condition can help individuals adapt better to the changes in vision and mobility. Gene testing is not possible because the gene has not yet been identified, but it is known to be located on chromosome 3.

▶ **DRPLA** *Dentato-rubro-pallido-luysian atrophy* is a rare condition named after the parts of the brain that are most affected by the disease. The gene responsible for DRPLA was identified in 1994 by a team of researchers in Japan. DRPLA is one of a group of neurologic disorders (which includes SCA1, SCA2, and MJD) caused by a particular kind of gene change known as "trinucleotide repeat expansion." It is not known why genes that are important in the nervous system are particularly prone to this kind of mutation, or exactly how these mutations cause diseases. But, because the gene mutations are similar, some of the answers to MJD and SCA1 may come from researchers studying DRPLA.

Most patients with DRPLA do not complain of "ataxia," because other symptoms are more prominent than the ataxia. However, ataxia may be apparent, particularly incoordination or "intention tremor" of the hands and arms. DRPLA commonly leads to many other abnormalities of limb movement, including involuntary movements (chorea and dystonia), tremor, and rigidity. Epilepsy (myoclonic seizures) may be present, particularly in those with onset in childhood or adolescence. The presence of epilepsy distinguishes DRPLA from the other common ataxias.

DRPLA, like SCA1 and MJD, is an autosomal dominant disease. A blood test can determine whether the gene change is present or not. Although no treatment will change the progression of symptoms, medications can help to control seizures, tremor, or rigidity.

▶ **Episodic ataxia (EA1 and EA2)**   There are two different types of episodic ataxia. Both are autosomal dominant disorders with symptoms usually beginning in the teenage years. In both disorders the most prominent symptoms, which are often brought on by exercise, are episodes of ataxia and dysarthria (unclear speech). In EA1 the episodes are usually very brief, lasting seconds to minutes, and are often associated with muscle twitching. In EA2 the episodes last longer (hours), are not associated with muscle twitches, and often nystagmus (involuntary eye movements) can be detected even between spells. EA2 can be treated and the spells controlled with acetazolamide, but this drug does not appear to help the episodes in EA1.

The gene responsible for EA1 was identified in 1994 by a team of researchers in Oregon. Because the disease is uncommon and because each family with the disorder has a different change in the gene, gene testing is not clinically available. The diagnosis is usually based on the patient history, the family history, neurologic examination, EMG findings (to characterize the muscle twitches), and response to acetazolamide.

The gene responsible for EA2 has not been identified, so gene testing is not possible, but it is known to be located on chromosome 19.

Hereditary early-onset ataxias

▶ **Friedreich's ataxia (FA)**   In the early 1860s, Dr. Nicholaus Friedreich described the disorder now known as *Friedreich's ataxia*. He noted that the disease did not affect the cerebellum as much as it did the nerve pathways in the spinal cord. Of the more than 10 hereditary ataxias, Friedreich's ataxia was the first to be distinguished from the other kinds of hereditary ataxia. The FA gene is located on chromosome 9 and was discovered in 1996 by researchers in Houston, Texas.

Friedreich's ataxia is an autosomal recessive (see glossary or chapter on genetics) form of ataxia. It typically begins in childhood or the teenage years, but occasionally symptoms don't appear until adulthood. Impaired ability to run is often the first sign of trouble. The child or school may complain of poor performance in sports or difficulty with activities that require good coordination.

As FA progresses, the affected individual finds walking and hand coordination more difficult. By the late teens or 20s, walking difficulties often progress to the point that individuals find it necessary or easier to use a wheelchair for mobility. After many years, the legs may become weak or develop contractures (tightening of the tendons, particularly in the ankles).

Other common symptoms of FA include high-arched feet (pes cavus) and curvature of the spine (scoliosis). For many people, high arches in the feet do not require any specific treatment, but curvature of the spine should be monitored by the general physician or orthopedic specialist. The growth spurt of adolescence may lead to worsening of scoliosis. As FA progresses, the speech becomes slower and indistinct, so the affected person learns to speak more carefully to be understood. The listener must also learn to take time to listen.

Most people with FA (about 90 percent) have an accelerated pulse, thickened heart wall, or changes on electrocardiogram (EKG). These changes may not be significant, but some patients do develop significant heart trouble or heart failure, which may require medication. Individuals with FA should have an EKG every two to three years (or more often if there are problems), and should remind their physician to examine the heart carefully during their annual physical examination.

Finally, about 15 to 20 percent of people with FA develop diabetes. This complication can usually be controlled easily with diet or medication, so anyone diagnosed with FA should be monitored carefully for symptoms of diabetes. Occasionally, diabetes is the first symptom of FA.

Other symptoms can occur in people with FA. Some of these symptoms may be related to FA, and some may not. Those who have FA and develop a new symptom or medical problem should be evaluated for the problem just as they would if they did not have FA.

The impact of FA on life activities is different for each person. Some individuals are able to perform everyday tasks such as bathing, dressing, grooming, and feeding for years even while relying on a wheelchair for mobility. Many people with FA live into their 40s and 50s and lead productive lives at home and work. Therefore, adequate planning for school, home life, job placement, and financial security are all very important for individuals or families affected by FA. (See chapters on job issues and financial planning for more information.)

Some people develop symptoms that resemble FA but don't fit the traditional pattern. For example, they may have symptoms starting after age 20, or reflexes still present on the neurologic examination. Now that the FA gene has been identified, it will be possible for a blood test to determine whether a patient truly has FA, or whether there are diseases similar to but genetically distinct from FA.

▶ **Ataxia telangiectasia (AT)** *Ataxia telangiectasia* (tee-lan-jack-tay-zha) is an autosomal recessive multisystem disease in which ataxia is a prominent and disabling symptom. The gene responsible for ataxia telangiectasia was identified in 1995 by a team of researchers in Israel. The affected gene appears to be one which is important in repairing damage to the DNA.

The neurologic symptoms of ataxia telangiectasia begin early in life with delays in acquiring motor milestones such as walking. Ataxia of gait is often noted when walking begins. In addition, some affected individuals have mild mental retardation or delays in acquiring cognitive (thinking) skills. The disorder of movement is complex and can include involuntary movements, slowness of movement, drooling, and dystonia (prolonged muscle contractions that may cause twisting and repetitive movements) as well as ataxia. Many patients have a characteristic abnormality of eye movements, called *oculomotor apraxia*, in which there is difficulty moving the eyes from side to side without also moving the head. As the condition progresses, peripheral neuropathy may develop, which leads to weakness or loss of sensation in the feet, legs, and hands. Speech and swallowing become more impaired. The neurologic symptoms progress slowly over a period of years. Patients usually require a wheelchair by the middle of the second decade.

Neurologic symptoms are only a part of the symptoms encountered by people with ataxia telangiectasia. Abnormal tangles of blood vessels (telangiectasias) in the conjunctiva (white part of the eye) and skin of the face, ears, or skin folds, may be detectable by the middle of the first decade. These signs might cause the pediatrician to suspect the diagnosis. As the disease progresses, some patients develop an "older" appearance because of skin changes usually associated with aging (loss of the fat layer under the skin, graying of the hair, etc.).

In AT the ability of the immune system to fight off infection and cancer is impaired. Most patients develop recurrent respiratory infections or skin infections in childhood. About 20 percent develop cancer of some type, most commonly leukemia or lymphoma. Susceptibility to infections and cancer is a major reason for the shortened life expectancy of people affected with AT. Survival after 30 years of age is uncommon in individuals with significant impairment of immune system function.

The diagnosis of AT might be relatively simple in people with all of the characteristic symptoms, but might be more difficult in those with fewer symptoms. Blood levels of a liver protein called alpha-fetoprotein are usually increased, and levels of certain immunoglobulins might be low. Neurologic and skin features of the disease might be noted on a physical exam. When more than one sibling is affected, an autosomal recessive disorder is likely.

There is no cure for AT, but treatment of infections and early detection of cancers can lead to a longer, healthier lifetime. Aggressive use of physical therapy, occupational therapy, speech therapy, and other resources can improve mobility, communication skills, and academic accomplishments.

Some researchers believe that carriers of an AT gene may be at an increased risk of developing cancer (although they do not develop AT symptoms). This is an area of intense interest and research at the time this book is being written. Anyone who may be a carrier of an AT gene (parent, sibling, or other relative of an affected individual) should contact his or her physician to find out the latest information about cancer risk and its effect on health management.

Other kinds of ataxia

There are a number of other genetic disorders that can produce ataxia as a prominent symptom. They fall roughly into three groups: structural disorders, metabolic disorders, and degenerative disorders.

▶ **Structural disorders** are those in which the cerebellum is not formed properly during development before birth. Commonly, individuals with these disorders have ataxia, abnormal eye movements, or other neurologic symptoms that are detectable at or shortly after birth. Disorders included in this category are Joubert's syndrome, Gillespie's syndrome, granule cell hypoplasia, and a number of other very rare conditions. Most of these conditions are autosomal recessive, which means there is a 25 percent chance for each new sibling of an affected individual to be born with the condition.

▶ **Metabolic disorders** are a large category of diseases that are caused by enzyme deficiencies. Most of these are autosomal recessive disorders. People who carry one copy of the abnormal gene are able to make enough of the enzyme to stay healthy, but affected individuals, who carry two copies of the abnormal gene, make so little enzyme that they develop symptoms.

Many metabolic disorders cause neurologic symptoms because the brain is particularly sensitive to the build-up of toxic products that the missing enzymes are supposed to break down, or to the absence of proteins or other products that the missing enzymes are supposed to create. Most patients with ataxia due to a metabolic disorder are not considered to have ATAXIA (the disease—as used in Chapter 1), but ataxia as a symptom of their metabolic disease.

Metabolic disorders that can result in episodes of ataxia include argininosuccinic aciduria, ornithine transcarbamylase deficiency, hyperornithemia, Hartnup disease, isovaleric acidemia and other organic acidemias, biotinidase deficiency, and disorders of pyruvate and lactate metabolism such as pyruvate dehydrogenase deficiency, Leigh's syndrome, and multiple carboxylase deficiency.

It is very important to diagnose these disorders properly, because symptoms can often be managed. In certain cases, altering the diet to avoid certain foods or taking large doses of specifically prescribed vitamins will prevent or improve symptoms.

Metabolic diseases that can cause progressive

ataxia include abetalipoproteinemia, hypobetalipoproteinemia, Vitamin E deficiency, leukodystrophies, Wilson's disease, mitochondrial encephalomyopathies, and Tay-Sach's disease. Proper diagnosis of these disorders can lead to appropriate genetic counseling, prenatal diagnosis in some cases, and dietary management in others.

▶ **Degenerative disorders**   Finally, other degenerative disorders of unknown origin can cause ataxia as a prominent feature. Many of these disorders have been given only descriptive names, since the underlying causes remain unknown. These disorders include ceroid lipofuscinosis, and ataxia with myoclonus, deafness, retinitis pigmentosa, optic atrophy (Behr's syndrome), cataracts and mental retardation (Marinesco-Sjögrens syndrome), and hypogonadism, among others. Each of these disorders is very rare, but once present in a family, they can affect several siblings.

What does GENETICS have to do with it?

MANY FORMS OF ATAXIA are genetic, which means they are caused by a defect in a certain gene that was there from the start of the person's life. Genetic diseases are not contagious—people can't "catch" or "give" genetic diseases through contact with others. Genetic, or hereditary, diseases can sometimes be passed from a parent to a child through the genes in the egg or sperm cell. Knowing how a specific genetic disease can be passed on in a family is important because different diseases have different genetic patterns.

Cells, chromosomes, and genes

Our bodies are made up of millions of *cells* of various types: heart cells, nerve cells, skin cells, egg cells, among many others. Every cell has numerous components working together almost like a microscopic factory.

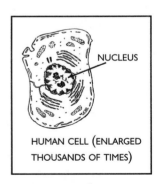

HUMAN CELL (ENLARGED THOUSANDS OF TIMES)

One essential component of every cell is the *nucleus*. The nucleus contains the *genes* that determine a person's characteristics.

The genes are assembled on spaghetti-like structures called *chromosomes*. We each have 23 pairs

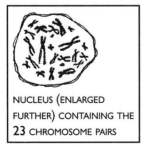

NUCLEUS (ENLARGED FURTHER) CONTAINING THE 23 CHROMOSOME PAIRS

of chromosomes (see illustration on next page). Nearly every cell in our bodies contains this double set of chromosomes. One member of each of the 23 chromosome pairs comes from the mother, and the other member of each pair comes from the father.

Humans have about 100,000 pairs of genes packaged in the 23 pairs of chromosomes. Thus, each chromosome contains 4,000 or more genes (the larger chromosomes probably have more, while the smaller chromosomes have fewer).

Cells, nuclei, and chromosomes are all large enough to be seen with a microscope. Genes are too small to be seen even with the most powerful microscope.

Genes are vitally important—without them, there would be no life. Genes provide the instructions to the cells for making the proteins or chemicals essential to life and health. Each gene also contains information that helps the cell to know when and how much of each chemical to make.

Although every body cell contains identical genes, some genes are only activated or "turned on" in certain cells or at certain times (for instance, there is no need for a gene responsible for eye color to be "turned on" in a heart cell, even though the gene is present in the heart cell). Some genes are only "turned on" during the time that an organ or tissue is being formed, or only during puberty, or only during times of stress. Other genes are always working because their function is necessary for the cell to survive or to perform its daily duties.

CHROMOSOMES

Chromosomes contain the genetic material that determines hereditary characteristics.

autosomes ——

Scientists number chromosomes according to their size: Chromosome 1 is the largest chromosome pair, and Chromosome 22 is the smallest chromosome pair. The first 22 chromosomes, called *autosomes*, are the same in males and females. The twenty-third chromosome pair looks different in males and females, and is important in determining the sex of a person. Females have two "X" chromosomes, while males have one "X" chromosome and one "Y" chromosome. The X and Y chromosomes are called the "sex chromosomes."

1
2
3
4
5
6
7
8
9
10
11
12
13
14
15
16
17
18
19
20
21
22

sex chromosomes ———————— X or Y

How genes cause diseases

All of us have genes that have little mistakes or variations in them. Most variations do not cause diseases. These harmless variations are called *polymorphisms*. An example of polymorphism is the different blood types (A, B, AB, and O). These different blood types are caused by polymorphisms (normal variations) in the ABO blood-type gene.

Occasionally, variations are significant enough to cause diseases, including ataxia. Disease-causing variations are called *mutations*. An example of a form of ataxia caused by a mutation is spinocerebellar ataxia type 1 (SCA1). It is caused by a mutation in the SCA1 gene, which changes the structure or function of the protein it directs the cell to make.

How genes cause ataxia

The genes responsible for hereditary ataxia are located in the nerve cells that make up the body's nervous system. The nervous system is very complex and requires precise connections among many, many cells. Numerous genes must function properly to allow the nervous system to 1) develop correctly, 2) function correctly so that the individual has good coordination and balance, and 3) stay healthy during the long lifetime of the individual. A mutation in a gene that is important in the development of the cerebellum might cause an abnormal appearance of the cerebellum and obvious ataxia at birth. A mutation in a gene that is important in the "daily work" of the cerebellum or spinal cord might allow the nervous system to develop normally and appear normal, but cause ataxia that presents itself later in life. And a mutation in a gene that is important in the "housekeeping" functions of the cerebellum or brainstem might result in slow deterioration of that part of the brain.

There are many genetic causes of ataxia. Over three hundred different genetic diseases, or "syndromes," have been described that include ataxia as a symptom. Unless there are other features of the disease to help the physician distinguish one syndrome from another, it may be very difficult to make a specific diagnosis. Ataxia due to one syndrome looks the same as ataxia due to any other syndrome or ataxia due to nongenetic causes. Some forms of ataxia can be distinguished by the way they are passed on in the family (known as the "genetic inheritance pattern"). The most important genetic inheritance patterns for people with ataxia are *autosomal dominant* and *autosomal recessive*.

Patterns of gene inheritance

▶ **Autosomal dominant inheritance pattern** The word *autosomal* means that the gene which causes the disease is located on one of the autosomes (an autosome is any of the chromosomes that are not sex chromosomes). Autosomal diseases are equally likely to affect males and females. *Dominant* means that the gene with the mutation (the disease gene) "dominates" over the normal copy of the gene (recall that genes come in pairs, one copy on each member of the chromosome pair). For autosomal dominant diseases, the presence of a normal gene is not enough to prevent the disease from developing.

The autosomal dominant inheritance pattern is seen in a number of the adult-onset hereditary cerebellar ataxias, including SCA1, SCA2, SCA3, SCA 5, SCA7, and DRPLA.

Some forms of familial spastic paraplegia (FSP) and essential tremor are also passed on this way.

HOW AN AUTOSOMAL DOMINANT DISORDER IS PASSED ON IN A FAMILY

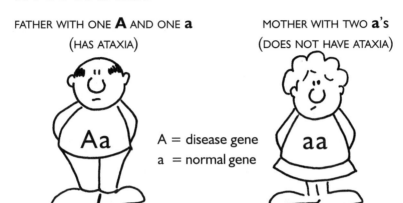

FATHER WITH ONE **A** AND ONE **a**
(HAS ATAXIA)

MOTHER WITH TWO **a**'s
(DOES NOT HAVE ATAXIA)

A = disease gene
a = normal gene

When a parent with autosomal dominant ataxia and a parent without ataxia produce offspring, each of the offspring will either inherit ataxia or not inherit ataxia depending on which genes are passed on.

Offspring who inherit one ataxia-causing gene will have ataxia.

Offspring who inherit two normal genes will not have ataxia.

Characteristics of autosomal dominant diseases:

- They have an equal chance of affecting males and females.
- Only one copy of a disease gene must be present to cause the disease.
- In general, all carriers of a disease gene will eventually develop symptoms of the disease.
- Anyone who does not carry a disease gene cannot pass the disease on to his or her children.
- Anyone who carries a disease gene can pass the disease on to his or her children (regardless of the sex of parent or child, and regardless of whether disease symptoms are present or how severe they are). For each child, the chance of receiving the disease gene is 50 percent.

The illustration on the previous page shows how an autosomal dominant disorder is passed on in a family. The ataxia-causing gene is labelled "A" and the normal version of the gene "a". The person with the ataxia has one copy of "A" and one copy of "a" (inherited from the unaffected parent). The unaffected partner, who does not come from an ataxia family, has two normal "a" genes. When the man makes sperm cells, either "A" or "a" (but not both) is put into each cell. When the woman makes egg cells, either "a" or the other "a" is put into each egg cell (they cannot be distinguished, and both are normal). When the sperm joins with the egg to make the first cell of the new fetus, the fetus has genes contributed by both the affected man and his unaffected partner. Half of the man's sperm cells have "A" and the other half have "a". Therefore, the chance that the fetus will inherit the "A" gene from the father and develop ataxia is one-half, or 50 percent. Any individual receiving the "a" gene from the affected father will not develop ataxia, but any individual receiving the "A" gene will develop ataxia. This 50 percent chance of inheriting the ataxia gene holds true for every child of an affected person. The chance that a particular child has inherited the ataxia gene is not changed in any way by the sex of the child, the sex or age of the parent, whether the previous child did or did not inherit the ataxia gene, or whether the affected parent has symptoms of ataxia or not.

As anyone who has ever flipped a coin knows, what is supposed to happen "on the average" half the time doesn't always happen that way. You can flip a coin six times and get "heads" all six times, or "heads" four times and "tails" twice. Similarly, a man or woman who carries a gene which causes dominant ataxia might have six children who all receive the ataxia gene, or who are all free of it, or any combination. However, each time that affected person has another child, the child's chance of having the ataxia gene is 50 percent.

The body has to accurately copy 100,000 genes in making each egg or sperm cell. Mistakes or gene changes happen during this process, and every so often a mistake occurs in an ataxia gene, causing ataxia to occur for the first time in the family. Once a gene mutation occurs, it can be passed on to the next generation. Many patients with ataxia have no family history of ataxia. It is difficult to determine whether these "sporadic" cases of ataxia are due to some nongenetic cause or whether they represent the first example in the family of a genetic disorder. Ataxia specialists have eagerly awaited the availability of ataxia gene tests to help them answer this question for their patients. If a person has a dominant mutation in an ataxia gene, each of his or her children has a 50 percent chance of inheriting the ataxia gene. If the disease is nongenetic, the children are no more likely than the general population to develop the disease.

▶ **Autosomal recessive inheritance pattern** The autosomal recessive inheritance pattern has some similarities and some differences when compared to autosomal dominant inheritance patterns. Autosomal recessive diseases are equally likely to occur in males and females because the responsible genes are located on an autosome pair. Unlike dominant diseases, it takes a "double dose" of a recessive disease gene to result in disease symptoms. People only develop disease symptoms when neither copy of a recessive gene is working properly. The most common recessive forms of ataxia are Friedreich's ataxia and ataxia telangiectasia. A number of less common forms of ataxia also appear to be autosomal recessive disorders.

Characteristics of autosomal recessive diseases:

- Males and females are equally likely to be affected.
- Two copies of the disease gene must be present before disease symptoms appear.
- Carriers of a single disease gene are generally normal, healthy individuals with no symptoms of the disease, but are able to pass the disease gene to their children.
- Both parents must be carriers of the disease gene in order to have an affected child; if both parents are disease gene carriers, the chance that any child of theirs will have a "double dose" of the disease gene and develop the disease is 25 percent.

Recessive disorders more commonly cause symptoms to begin in childhood rather than adulthood (although for reasons which are not well understood, symptoms are not necessarily present at birth or in infancy).

To get a double-dose of a disease gene, a child must receive one copy of the disease gene from each parent. Most of the time, neither parent knows that he or she has a recessive disease gene until a child with a recessive disorder appears. Even then, the genetic nature of the disorder may not be appreciated, and the child's symptoms may be attributed to other causes. Often it is not until a second child has the same disorder that a genetic cause is suspected.

How did the unsuspecting parents get recessive disease genes, and how did they happen to have the same recessive disease gene? Because a single recessive disease gene causes no symptoms, it is possible for it to be passed on in the family for generations without being recognized. Some recessive genes are quite common, and others are quite rare. For instance, a gene which causes a severe blood disease called sickle-cell anemia when present in a double dose turns out to be very common in African countries where malaria is a common disease—because a *single dose* of the sickle-cell gene helps to protect against malaria. Thus, people who have a single copy of the sickle-cell gene live longer than people who don't because they don't develop malaria.

As far as we know, having a single copy of an ataxia gene doesn't protect against anything, and ataxia genes are not common in most ethnic groups in America. However, the Friedreich's ataxia gene appears to be more common in people of French-Canadian origin than in other ethnic groups. A man and woman of French-Canadian descent who have children might have a higher chance of having a child with Friedreich's than a couple of a different ethnic background because both the man and the woman are a little more likely than average to have a single copy of the Friedreich's disease gene. A man

HOW AN AUTOSOMAL RECESSIVE DISORDER IS PASSED ON IN A FAMILY

FATHER WITH ONE **F** AND ONE **f**
(DOES NOT HAVE ATAXIA)

MOTHER WITH ONE **f** AND ONE **F**
(DOES NOT HAVE ATAXIA)

F = normal gene
f = disease gene

The above parents each have one recessive ataxia-causing gene. Each of their offspring could inherit one of four possible gene combinations:

F from father, **f** from mother (child does not have ataxia but can pass disease gene on to future children)

f from father, **F** from mother (child does not have ataxia but can pass disease gene on to future children)

F from father, **F** from mother (child does not have ataxia and has no disease gene to pass on to future children)

f from father, **f** from mother (double-dose of ataxia-causing gene means child will have ataxia and will pass disease gene on to all future children) and woman who are related to each other (distant cousins, for example) are also more likely to have in common the same disease genes. The same recessive disease gene can, uncommonly, happen to be present in an unrelated man and woman.

The illustration on the previous page shows how recessive genes are passed on in families. In this case, we will call "F" the normal Friedreich's gene and "f" the altered gene. An unsuspecting man and woman, both perfectly normal in every way, are both carriers of one F and one f. When the father makes sperm cells, he puts either the F or the f but not both into each sperm cell. The mother likewise puts either F or f into the eggs. When the sperm fertilizes the egg to form the new baby, there are four possible combinations of sperm and egg: FF, Ff, fF, and ff. The children who receive FF, Ff, or Ff are all normal, but the Ff or fF children can pass the recessive gene on to *their* children. The children who receive ff have a double-dose of the disease gene and will develop Friedreich's ataxia.

Only one out of four possible sperm/egg combinations results in an affected child, so the chance that a child born to this couple will develop Friedreich's ataxia is one-fourth, or 25 percent. As noted for dominant disorders, one-fourth does not mean that exactly one of four children will develop the disease. It simply means that each child's chance of having the disease gene is 25 percent. The parents and the children with Ff and fF are all "carriers" of the disease gene. Carriers usually do not have symptoms of any disease and should not be considered to be "sick" in any way, but they can pass on the disease gene to the next generation.

The National Ataxia Foundation (see Resources section) offers a pamphlet on *Gene Testing for Ataxia*. It explains what testing can accomplish, who should consider it, and where testing is done.

YOU
and your
DOCTOR

Building your health team

Medical management of ataxia

Building your HEALTH TEAM

Getting a diagnosis

The first step in getting a diagnosis when you have ataxia is recognizing that there is a problem. The second step is finding a physician you trust and with whom you can communicate freely. You can

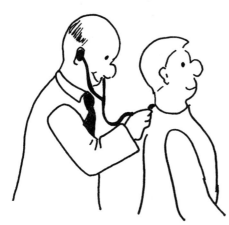

help the physician by being honest about your symptoms (all of them), as accurate as possible about the dates and details of your medical history, and by collecting information about your family history.

The physician will examine you, and will usually order some blood tests and an MRI scan of

your brain. This will help to ensure that your symptoms are not caused by medical or neurologic conditions which can cause ataxia. There are many possible causes of ataxia, from vitamin deficiencies to a stroke, so the correct diagnosis may not be obvious immediately.

You may be referred to a specialist, or you may independently seek a second opinion from a specialist. A neurologist is often the most helpful specialist at diagnosing the cause of ataxia. Even an experienced neurologist, however, may suspect other diagnoses such as multiple sclerosis or Parkinson's disease rather than one of the ataxias, because the ataxias are uncommon.

Even if the diagnosis is sporadic or hereditary ataxia, it may not be possible to make a more specific diagnosis. Only specialized gene tests can make specific diagnoses such as SCA1 or MJD.

At the time of this writing (1996), gene tests for ataxia are very new and may only be known to neurologists specializing in movement disorders, ataxia, or degenerative diseases. Your physician or a genetic counselor can help you to know if a gene test is appropriate for you. The National Ataxia Foundation or a genetic counselor can help you find out where and how to have a gene test.

If you are diagnosed with ataxia, it is important to learn as much as you can about the disease and how it will affect you now and in the future, because ataxia does not go away!

Bring a list of questions to ask your physician. Some important questions might include: Can I work? Do I have any physical limitations? Are my symptoms mild or severe? Can I eat a regular diet? Should I exercise? Is there a medicine I should take? What is this medicine for, and what side effects can it cause? Whom should I call in an emergency?

The more knowledgeable you are about ataxia, and the better you understand and can describe your symptoms, the better your physician will be able to treat you.

Building a relationship with your doctor

Receiving a diagnosis of ataxia can make you feel as if you are losing control of your life. One way to feel more in control is to take an active role in your health care. Think of yourself and your medical caregivers as a team working to manage your symptoms in a way that will help you get the most out of your life even with ataxia.

Becoming informed is important to being an active player on your health care team. Learn about ataxia and the particular kind of ataxia you have. Reading this manual all the way through is a good beginning. It provides basic information and can lead you to many helpful resources.

Having a good relationship with your physician can increase your health care team's effectiveness. When you find a physician you feel comfortable with, make an effort to build a good relationship. You might also want to identify and work on areas of the relationship that need improvement. See the Resource section or check the library for books on building healthy doctor-patient relationships.

Choosing the right doctor for your team

It's a good idea to choose one main physician to supervise your overall health care. He or she might be a general family practitioner or a specialist such as a neurologist.

Because ataxia is an uncommon disorder, many physicians will not be experienced with it. This may not matter, since many symptoms that accompany ataxia would be treated the same whether the ataxia is present or not.

Look for a physician who shows interest in learning about ataxia if he or she is not already familiar with it. You might offer to provide printed information from the National Ataxia Foundation and other sources as a starting point.

Your goal should be to have a primary physician you trust and feel comfortable with, who will:

- supervise your overall health maintenance, which might be more complicated than average by the fact that you have ataxia;
- make an effort to understand the specific ways your ataxia is affecting you;
- prescribe treatments, when appropriate, that will help you feel better and function better;
- be aware of the special concerns of ataxia patients (such as possible atypical responses to medications) when treating specific symptoms, and anticipate potential problems;
- make referrals to other health professionals when needed.

Medical specialists and other health professionals

With appropriate education, careful medical management of specific symptoms, and timely involve-

ment of other specialists, your quality of life can be improved considerably.

Progressive forms of ataxia eventually impact the functioning of many body systems. Therefore, it is likely that you will be referred to other medical specialists from time to time for therapy, consultations, or advice.

The following list describes some of the health professionals who might participate in your care (depending on the kind of ataxia that you have):

- *internist*—may specialize in general internal medicine or a subspecialty

Internist subspecialties include:

cardiologist—specializes in diagnosing and treating heart problems

gastroenterologist—specializes in treating disorders of the gastrointestinal organs, which include the digestive tract, liver, biliary tract, and pancreas

nephrologist—specializes in kidney disorders

pulmonary specialist—treats symptoms and diseases associated with or affecting the lungs

- *neurologist*—specializes in diagnosing and treating diseases of the nervous system, including the brain, spinal cord, and peripheral nerves (since ataxia affects the cerebellum of the brain, a neurologist often diagnoses and oversees the care of ataxia patients)

- *ophthalmologist*—specializes in diagnosing and treating eye disorders

- *orthopedic surgeon*—uses surgical means to prevent or correct musculoskeletal deformities

- *urologist*—specializes in disorders of the urinary tract

- *physical therapist*—uses therapeutic properties of exercise, heat, cold, electricity, ultraviolet radiation, and massage to improve circulation, strengthen muscles, encourage return of motion, and help individuals learn to perform the activities of daily living

- *occupational therapist*—develops individual programs to increase skills for self-care, work, and leisure; promotes independence and quality of life through task and environment adaptations

- *physiatrist*—physician who specializes in rehabilitation medicine and often works with or supervises a team of occupational or physical therapists

- *speech pathologist*—develops individual programs to improve communication skills for people with speech impairments; evaluates and recommends treatments for swallowing disorders
- *genetic counselor*—specializes in hereditary diseases, explaining genetic principles and counseling about genetic risks and testing
- *social worker*—assists families in goal-setting and coordinates appropriate community and government resources to meet individual and family needs

Strategies for effective team communication

You probably have many unanswered questions if you have recently been diagnosed with ataxia. Between doctor visits, you might wish to write down your questions and concerns as they occur to you. Be aware that it will not be possible to cover a long list of symptoms and questions in a single visit. Trying to do so will result in frustration for both you and your doctor, and the most important issues might get overlooked.

Rather than producing a written list during the appointment, bring up two or three issues that are of the most immediate concern to you. Then let your doctor know that you have many more questions on your list and ask how he or she would like to handle them. The doctor might agree to look at the list then or at a later time, or might suggest scheduling another appointment, perhaps a longer one, to discuss your concerns.

If you consistently feel you are being rushed or are not getting adequate information, bring it up in a tactful manner. If you and your doctor are unable to resolve communication problems, or if he or she seems insensitive to your needs, it might be time to consider finding another doctor.

Medical schools place much emphasis on diagnosis *and cure*. Some doctors feel frustrated in dealing with diseases they can't cure. You might wish to make a point of letting your doctor know when a treatment or recommendation—or even his or her caring manner—proves helpful to you.

Your role during your medical appointment is to provide information about your symptoms honestly and concisely. If medicines are prescribed, ask what they are for and what the potential side effects might be. To be sure you understand what the dosage is, try repeating the information back to the doctor, or ask to have it written down. Understand that you are responsible for taking medicines properly and for informing the doctor of any side effects.

It is worth the time and effort it takes for you and your doctor to build a relationship of openness, caring, and mutual respect. Such a relationship can be a powerful factor in your own physical and emotional well-being.

MEDICAL management of ataxia

AT THIS TIME, the goals of treatment of ataxia are to improve the quality of life. For certain types of ataxia, such as ataxia due to Vitamin E deficiency, specific treatment of the underlying problem may improve the ataxia itself. But for most kinds of ataxia, the main focus of medical treatment is on identifying symptoms related to or caused by the ataxia, and treating those symptoms.

Your physician can help you to anticipate potential health problems before they happen. He or she can also involve specialists, such as physical therapists, speech pathologists, genetic counselors, and social workers, to help address the many needs that you and your family may have. Through education, timely involvement of other specialists, and medical treatment of specific symptoms, the quality of life of any person with ataxia can be improved considerably.

There are no cures for any of the ataxias. Brain transplants or brain surgery, which are sometimes performed for individuals with Parkinson's disease, have not been studied and are not currently recommended for individuals with ataxia. Treatments directed against the immune system, which are helpful for people with multiple sclerosis, would not be expected to help people with ataxia and should be avoided. As scientists learn more about the changes in the brain that lead to ataxia, they are working to develop new drugs that can slow down or stop the progression of symptoms. So far, no "ataxia drugs" have been found effective or approved by the Federal Drug Administration for use in the United States, but this may change over the next few years.

Even though there is not a cure, a number of drugs and treatments are available to manage the common symptoms that people with ataxia notice.

Some common symptoms and their treatments:

▶ **fatigue** Can be caused by medical problems unrelated to ataxia, by depression, sleep disturbances, overwork, or the neurologic disease itself. Correct diagnosis of the underlying cause of fatigue is important, as is taking extra time to rest or sleep. Many people use mild stimulants such as caffeine to combat fatigue, and occasionally physicians prescribe stimulants such as pemoline or methylphenidate, or antidepressants such as sertraline (Zoloft) for patients with excessive fatigue. When fatigue is due to ataxia, however, rest is probably a more appropriate treatment than stimulant drugs, for most individuals.

▶ **sleep disturbance** Disturbed sleep can have many causes, some related and some unrelated to ataxia. A particular sleep disorder, called REM behavior disorder, is more common in people with sporadic OPCA. This disorder, in which patients act out their dreams while they are asleep, can usually be treated successfully with clonazepam. Insomnia (difficulty falling or staying asleep) can often be improved by changing the sleep habits, or by the careful use of medications such as trazodone, tricyclic antidepressants, or sedative/hypnotic drugs such as zolpidem. All drugs that help with sleep can have significant side effects, and some can be addictive and should not be used on a long-term basis.

▶ **tremor**   There are different kinds of tremor; the kind of tremor that is most common in ataxia is an intention tremor. Occasionally, people with ataxia have one of the other kinds of tremor (resting tremor, postural tremor, or action tremor). While there are no medications for intention tremor, anti-Parkinsonian drugs such as carbidopa/levodopa or trihexyphenidyl can improve resting tremor, and propranolol, clonazepam, or primidone can improve postural or action tremor.

▶ **spasticity (stiffness)**   Not all stiffness is caused by spasticity, which is a specific neurologic symptom. If a therapist or physician has identified that a person has spasticity, a number of treatments can be helpful, including stretching, heat, and medication with antispasticity drugs such as baclofen or diazepam.

▶ **anxiety/depression**   Depression and anxiety are very common with all types of ataxia. While reassurance, friendship, or counseling can help with mild episodes of depression, severe episodes might require treatment with antidepressant medications. A number of antidepressants are available, so treatment can be tailored to an individual's specific needs. Likewise, a number of antianxiety medications are available for people whose anxiety interferes with their ability to function normally.

▶ **aches and pains**   Pain is not commonly caused by the ataxia itself, but people with ataxia are not protected from getting the normal aches and pains that people without ataxia get. Because of awkward positioning of the body or limbs, or falls, people with ataxia may be a little more likely to develop joint pains or bruises than others. In general, people with ataxia can use any drug to treat aches and pains that people without ataxia can use, including aspirin, acetaminophen, and nonsteroidal anti-inflammatory drugs such as ibuprofen. Like all medications, these should be used carefully since they can all be dangerous if used in high doses over a long time.

▶ **fever, infections**   Except for those with ataxia telangiectasia, individuals with ataxia do not have a higher risk of infections until very late in the disease, when choking increases the chance of lung infections, or immobility increases the chance of lung, urinary, or skin infections. However, most people with ataxia notice that their ataxia symptoms are worse when they are sick with some type of infection. In fact, for some, an abrupt change in ataxia symptoms may be the first sign of an infection. The treatment of fever and infections in people with ataxia is the same as it is in people without ataxia.

NOTE: This list does not include all the symptoms that people with ataxia can get, only some of the more common ones. It is important for people with ataxia to have good general medical care, because ataxia does not protect one from having the usual health problems that anyone can get, such as tooth abscesses, farsightedness, ulcers, or breast cancer. It is important to have a good relationship with one main or primary doctor so that you feel free to discuss your symptoms frankly.

An important warning about medications

While medications may be very helpful in reducing symptoms and improving the quality of life for someone with ataxia, all medications can have side effects. People with ataxia tend to be more sensitive than others to any drugs that cause drowsiness,

dizziness, blurred vision, or confusion. Make sure before you take any medication (and this warning includes over-the-counter medications!) that you discuss with the physician or pharmacist why you are taking the medication, what benefits to expect, what side effects to watch out for, what to do if you accidentally miss a dose or experience a side effect, what the pre-

scribed dose is, and whether it might interact with any other medicine you are taking. Many people with ataxia take half of the prescribed dose of a new medicine for the first time or two so they can get used to the drug and avoid unpleasant side effects.

What about vitamins, minerals, and herbal remedies?

If your ataxia is caused by a specific vitamin deficiency, such as Vitamin E deficiency, then treatment with large doses of that vitamin may be the most specific and best treatment. If your ataxia is *not* caused by Vitamin E deficiency, there is no reason to think that large doses of Vitamin E will be helpful. If you are eating a regular and healthy diet, you probably do not require vitamin supplements. If you think your diet is inadequate or missing certain vitamins, a daily multivitamin tablet will certainly not hurt. For most vitamins, "mega-doses" are not necessary, and they can be dangerous with certain vitamins.

If a moderate dose of a particular vitamin, mineral, or herb makes you feel better in some way, it may be worth the cost as long as it is doing no harm. Be wary of advertisements reporting miracle cures or products which are said to treat or cure many different unrelated medical diseases or conditions. When in doubt, consult with your physician or pharmacist about new treatments you are considering.

Managing your life with ataxia

Coping strategies

Coping with changing relationships

Adapting for daily living

Mobility

Exercising

Nutrition, eating and choking

Speaking

Job issues

Financial planning

Having fun

Coping STRATEGIES

ATAXIA DOESN'T cause physical pain. But ataxia can cause a different kind of pain—the mental and psychological anguish that comes with unanswered questions, stares of curious people, the fear of choking, and the progression of the disease. How do you cope with these realities?

Accepting your feelings

A person facing ataxia may experience many different emotions: anger, anxiety, denial, embarrassment, fear, frustration, grief, guilt, helplessness, isolation, and uncertainty. Added to these emotions may be apathy, altered relationships, difficulty communicating, family conflicts, and loss of freedom, privacy, and self-esteem that come with the progressing disease. These are the roadblocks that must be overcome by your coping skills—no medicine can take them away.

It is important to remember that every person experiences feelings like these. They are unavoidable responses to life-altering events. Not only do intense emotions affect the person who has ataxia, but they also affect family members and friends, and individuals at risk for hereditary ataxia. To make matters more complicated, different or conflicting emotions may be present at the same time.

The two least expensive and most helpful coping

aids are time and companionship. Sometimes you simply need time to think about your situation, to consider options, opportunities, and solutions. It is equally important to have another person you trust, with whom you can share your feelings or concerns. This person could be a relative, a close friend, a clergyperson, or a trained counselor. Whether you are coping "normally" or "abnormally" depends upon whether you are able to function well while you are working on coping with ataxia.

You may find there are times when you cope well by yourself, but there are other times when you need the emotional support of another person to get you through a difficult time. Do not be embarrassed or afraid to seek help when you need it. Most of us have difficulty accepting illness. We don't like being faced with our limitations; to some, limitations suggest failure, which we all want to avoid. Often, it is not the physical symptoms that cause the most distress, but the feelings of being "different." However, by allowing yourself to accept the reality of your "differences" or "limitations," you can open new dimensions of living, growing, and relating.

Think about the differences between "living with *ataxia*," "living *with* ataxia," and "*living* with ataxia." When the diagnosis of ataxia is first made, it controls your life. As you learn more about the disease and understand how it affects you, you come to live side by side with it. Eventually, as you become fully adapted to life with ataxia and accustomed to your routines, you can once again begin to *live,* and your ataxia fades in comparison with your spiritual, emotional, and physical achievements and enjoyments. Life after ataxia will be different from life before ataxia, but some of the changes may be wonderful!

Taking control by planning for the future

For some people, careful planning for the future is a part of coping with a chronic illness. It can be very satisfying to know that you have made financial arrangements for your family for after you die, to have a will in place, or to know that your family understands how you wish to be cared for during your last days. Discuss these things if you want to—otherwise, it becomes very easy to put them off for weeks, months, or years. For additional information, see the chapter on financial planning.

Begin building your own resources list

books   There are many books about living with chronic disease that can help you cope. Although these books may not address some of the problems that are unique to ataxia, some of the emotions and daily struggles are similar. See the Resources section and check your library or bookstore for books on coping that might be helpful to you. See the Resource section for information on doing your own library research.

professional services   Through your physician or your county Family Services Agency, you can gain access to social workers, psychologists, rehabilitation counselors, or family counselors.

spiritual guidance   Talk to a clergyperson at your church or synagogue, or in the hospital chaplaincy department.

support groups   A support group is a good place to build your ataxia management skills and to make friends. There are, in many communities, ataxia support groups affiliated with the National Ataxia Foundation. In other communities, support groups for people with multiple sclerosis, head injury, or Parkinson's disease may be helpful to you. If you have Internet access, there are ataxia support groups online. A good starting point on the Internet is at *www.ataxia.org*—this is the home page of the National Ataxia Foundation.

Coping with changing
RELATIONSHIPS

IN INTERVIEWS with thousands of patients, Linda Hanner, author and speaker on patient issues, found that many people with serious illnesses say the most painful aspect of their situation is the lack of understanding from loved ones. She explains that it is important to realize that every person who is close to someone diagnosed with serious illness experiences grief over the losses created by the situation and that each person has unique ways of coping with that grief.

Hurt is often expressed as anger or defensiveness. Sometimes it is easier for people to at least temporarily deny the reality of illness rather than face the implications. Illness often brings out unexpected strengths and weaknesses. It is important to concentrate on the strengths rather than the weaknesses.

Hanner offers these suggestions for people who are concerned about the effects their debilitating illness will have on personal relationships:

- Don't expect your spouse to fulfill all of your needs. An interview with a woman who has a chronic illness revealed an important insight:

  "Before the illness, I had certain expectations of my husband. Eventually, I realized that he couldn't fulfill all the roles I wanted him to. He ended up doing what he was best at, which was taking the problem-solving role...I learned to lean on my friends for emotional support when I needed it. The illness really brought out our differences, yet I realized that it didn't mean he didn't love me or that we couldn't handle the situation together."

• Talk out your feelings and encourage family members to do the same. Very often anger at the illness comes out as anger at each other. Talking out feelings helps identify their true source and leads to more productive solutions.

• Be willing to forgive. A willingness to forgive is probably a key ingredient to the survival of any relationship.

• Encourage friends and family members to continue participating in activities you previously enjoyed together, even if you can no longer always join in. Remember to ask them how they are doing and allow them to "unload" on you occasionally.

Sex and sexuality

Many people consider a fulfilling sexual life an important part of their overall happiness. What makes for a fulfilling sexual life or experience may vary considerably from one person to the next. A chronic condition like ataxia can affect sexual desires, performance, opportunities or satisfaction in many ways. This section offers general information and suggestions, but if you have concerns about your ataxia as it relates to your sexuality, you'll want to discuss those concerns with a trusted physician or counselor.

While the symptom of ataxia does not relate in any way to the ability to have an erection or an orgasm, some of the additional neurologic symptoms that some people with ataxia develop can affect sexual function. Anyone who has bladder disturbance for neurologic reasons can have sexual dysfunction too, because similar nerves are involved in both processes. Sometimes neuropathy affects the nerves involved in bowel, bladder, and sexual control.

Sexual function can be affected indirectly in people with ataxia for a number of reasons. Fatigue, depression, altered self-image, pain, and slowness of movement can all affect sexual desire and performance.

Finally, it is always possible that changes in sexual function in a person with ataxia have nothing to do with the ataxia, but are related to some other medical problem such as diabetes, enlargement of the prostate, or, in women, bladder prolapse or other changes related to menopause. A number of commonly used medications can affect sexual function. For these reasons, it is always appropriate to have a medical evaluation if there are disturbing changes in sexual function.

Relationships will change over the years with or without ataxia, but the onset of ataxia is likely to trigger a number of changes in even the most stable of relationships. The loss of physical strength, loss of ability to work and drive, and loss of ability to control body functions as the ataxia progresses are challenges for the affected individual and for the partner. Sometimes the partner becomes a caregiver. Fear of the future, grief about the changes that have already taken place and a feeling of loss are all very common in both the affected person and the partner. It is not surprising if sexual relationships are unsatisfying during this time of physical and emotional upheaval. However, if sexual relationships can be resumed in a way that is satisfying to both partners, it can be an enormous boost to the relationship. Conversely, satisfactory sexual relationships usually reflect a healthy overall partnership.

If you have ataxia and you feel that your sexual function is affected either because of physical changes or because of emotional changes, talk to your partner, your doctor or a counselor about the problem. Sometimes there are simple physical problems that can be treated. If depression is affecting sexual desire or function in you or your partner, counseling or medication can help. A counselor may be able to help you and you partner work together to understand what the underlying problems are and to communicate your needs to each other.

It is possible for people with ataxia to have a happy and fulfilling sex life. It just may take a little extra effort!

ADAPTING
for daily living

ACCESSIBILITY TO HOUSING and adaptations for safety and ease are very important, especially for those who rely on a wheelchair. If you are planning to buy a house or are looking for an apartment, keep accessibility and adaptability in mind. Some cities have apartment complexes especially designed for wheelchair living, but these are few and often have long waiting lists for occupancy.

People with neurological or physical handicaps often find that everyday activities can be made easier by making modifications to the home or work environment and learning new, adaptive techniques for accomplishing tasks.

New ways to get things done

If you live in a house which is not completely accessible, and you use or anticipate using a wheelchair, you might need some home modifications. Health care institutions (particularly rehabilitation units) or agencies dealing with handicapped housing can help assess your house and identify financial resources.

On your own, you can begin to evaluate your home and daily activities. Many relatively simple modifications can be made to home or apartment in order to make everyday tasks easier to accomplish.

It's best if bedroom, bathroom, and living areas

are on the same floor. If there are stairs, consider installing a stair lift.

bedroom   Side rails for the bed may contribute to a feeling of security. You may find it helpful to use a "transfer board" for sliding from bed to wheelchair with or without assistance. Floor-to-ceiling poles in the bedroom and elsewhere throughout the home can provide support for standing or in transferring to and from a wheelchair.

Getting dressed can be made easier with aids such as elastic shoelaces, hook-and-loop tape (Velcro) closures instead of buttons or hooks, and a "dressing stick" to help pull on clothing. It is important that you dress yourself and do as much of your own self-care as possible, even if it takes longer. It is good exercise and will enable you to maintain your independence in this area as well as helping your self-image. If you are unable to dress while standing or sitting, try getting dressed in bed, rolling from side to side.

bathroom   Is the doorway wide enough for wheelchair access? Special hinges can be purchased and installed on regular doors to allow an additional couple of inches. Grab bars are helpful by the toilet and bathtub. Side rails for the tub can provide needed support. Lifts for transfers to the bathtub or toilet may be obtained from hospital equipment suppliers and rental agencies.

kitchen   Food preparation and clean-up can be made easier by modifying countertop heights to provide lower work areas, opening space under the sink to accommodate a wheelchair, building storage shelves at the back of counters for easy reaching, and providing wheelchair space at one side of the stove for easier oven access.

Your physician or occupational therapist can recommend special implements and aids for eating, which might include:

- Holders for glasses or cups to prevent their being tipped over
- Covers for cups to prevent spilling while carrying them
- Long, sturdy drinking straws, so you don't need to pick up the cup or glass
- Non-skid mats to hold plates in place (or use a damp towel)
- Plates with a rim or sides
- "Rocker knives" to assist in cutting food
- Built-up handles on silverware for a more secure grasp
- Suction cups for plates, glasses, etc.

Conserving your energy

Ataxia takes away some of your energy, so plan your daily activities in a way that conserves energy. Lean against the counter for support while doing dishes or other standing activities. There are many household chores which you can do while sitting, such as ironing, mixing foods, or washing dishes. Try using a standard mixer instead of a portable one, and a bowl holder to avoid spilling. Allow dishes to air dry in a drainer, or use a dishwasher if you have one. Lightweight utensils are much easier to handle, and nonbreakable dishes and glassware are better.

It's important that you don't become exhausted. Space heavy tasks throughout the day or week rather than attempting to do too much at once. Avoid rushing—set priorities for what you must do, and let others take a share of the responsibilities. Simplify your tasks as much as possible.

Arrange your work and storage areas within

normal reach. Avoid unnecessary bending, lifting or carrying of heavy items. Push things rather than lifting whenever possible, bending at the knees to avoid back strain. Use a wheeled serving cart to transport items. If you use a walker, attach bags to it for carrying things. A backpack might be useful for lightweight items when you need both hands free to use canes or crutches.

These are just a few suggestions to start you thinking of ways to plan and simplify daily activities to fit your individual needs. Rehabilitation centers and occupational therapists can offer you other ideas and information about self-help aids and how to order them.

Brochures and information books and booklets on home modifications for the handicapped are available from various service agencies and from the U.S. Government Printing Office. Send your request for a free publications catalog to the Government Printing Office at North Capitol and H Streets NW, Washington, DC 20401. Also, check your local library for information resources on housing and adaptive equipment for people with disabilities. Ask the librarian to help you find the information you need.

MOBILITY—there's more than one way to get from here to there

THERE ARE a great many types of mobility aids available to help you maintain independence. You'll need to assess your particular needs and consult with your physician and/or physical therapist for assistance in choosing the appropriate devices. Purchasing sources include hospital supply or orthotic dealers and medical equipment catalogues.

Walking aids for balance and support

Canes or crutches may be helpful as balance and walking become more precarious. There are a variety of styles, including single canes, quad canes with four small feet that provide extra stability, underarm crutches, and forearm crutches.

Ankle supports of various types may provide increased stability for walking. Some people with ataxia find that high-top shoes, boots, ankle-foot orthoses (braces), or shoe inserts are beneficial.

A walker may be indicated to assist in balance and walking. The conventional four-poster walker requires adequate coordination to pick it up and move it forward every step or two.

Wheels on the front can make it easier to propel the walker, but care should be taken that it does not roll away from the user. Hand-grip brakes can be a good safety feature. Some styles of walkers fold and have seats for resting, and some can be fitted with a basket or tray to carry things.

Parallel bars may be useful. There are adjustable and electric models. Some can be folded against a hallway wall when not in use.

Other supports that can be useful for getting around include stair rails and wall rails. Strategically placed grab bars can provide helpful support.

Wheelchairs

When it is advantageous to use a wheelchair, your physician or physical therapist can guide your choice of styles. There are both manual and electric wheelchairs, many with a lightweight design convenient for traveling. Battery-operated scooters are favored by some.

Wheelchair accessories are designed to add convenience and comfort. Look for specially designed cushions and back inserts, brake extensions for easier operation, cup holders, and baskets or bags for carrying things. Many wheelchair users find that open-fingered bike gloves protect the hands and provide traction while pushing a manual chair.

Specially equipped vans are a convenient alternative to the difficulties that people who use wheelchairs often confront in trying to use a regular automobile. Vans are available with manual and hydraulic lifts. Extended lifts can make trans-

fer easier. Accessories include automatic door openers with remote control, dropped floors or overhead bubbles. An economical approach to acquiring a suitable vehicle might be to custom fit a stripped van to your specific needs.

Other transportation

Local community services often include transportation for people with disabilities. Some larger communities, such as the Minneapolis/St. Paul area, have a special part of their public transportation system designed for people with disabilities. In the Twin Cities, it is called Metro Mobility, and is coordinated through the Metropolitan Transit Commission (MTC).

Planning to travel by air? Airlines will often allow an attendant or companion to accompany a disabled person at a reduced fare.

Driving laws for people with disabilities

Laws concerning drivers with disabilities may vary from state to state. Generally, the laws have these basic features:

- An applicant for a driver's license must answer the question of whether he or she has a physical impairment, convulsive disorder, history of blackouts, strokes, etc., on the license application.
- If the answer to this question is yes, the applicant must explain. He or she may be required to take a driving test. It may be necessary to have your physician fill out a questionnaire.
- Renewal evaluations are judged on an individual basis, depending on the physician's recommendations and the decision of the State Driver Evaluation Unit. Further certifications of ability to

continue to drive may be required from a physician from time to time. The driver's test does not have to be repeated unless there is a record of accidents or driving problems that need to be reevaluated.

• People with special hand controls, special mirrors or other special equipment on their vehicles must re-take the permit test, take a driver's instruction course, and then take the road driving test.

• The physician's statement for the handicapped may be obtained from the State Department of Transportation (or Public Safety), and must be filled out to certify that the applicant is judged able to drive.

• Certain rehabilitation agencies offer handicapped driver education evaluation and training programs. Contact your local handicapped advocacy agencies for programs near you.

• Handicapped license plates are available in most states for people with permanent disabilities. The main advantage of these plates is to alert other drivers to be aware that a handicapped person is driving the vehicle. Usually the driver must have non-use of the appendages (necessitating crutches, etc.) to qualify for the plates. Contact your state automobile licensing agency for details.

• In some states, handicapped parking permits are available to allow the car to be parked in designated handicapped parking areas which are more convenient and accessible. If the handicapped person is the driver, a driving test may be required if one hasn't already been required for the license. A handicapped parking permit may also be available for a vehicle even if the handicapped person is not the driver. A physician must provide a statement of need and complete part of the application. Contact your State Department of Motor Vehicles for information.

EXERCISING — it's a good thing!

EXERCISE IS particularly important for people who have ataxia. Those who are able to develop and follow an exercise program usually comment that it helps their mental attitude in addition to improving their physical condition. Make it your goal to establish an exercise program that is stimulating, enjoyable and challenging.

The best type of exercises are aerobic exercises. Examples are walking, running, bicycling, skiing, swimming, and rowing (but not weight lifting or sprinting).

Benefits of aerobic exercises

- They use several different muscle groups at once.
- They speed up the heart and breathing rate. (To get the most from an aerobic exercise, continue the exercise for at least several minutes.)
- They help you maintain muscle tone and power. (They are not designed to make you bigger like a weight lifter or body builder.)
- They force you to stretch the muscles out, which makes them relaxing to many people. This is of added benefit to anyone with ataxia who also has some stiffness.

Sticking with it

People who make exercise a regular part of their schedule or routine are more likely to succeed in sticking with their program over the long term. To be of the most benefit, exercise sessions should take place at least three times a week. Many health clubs have aerobics or fitness classes that can provide an incentive to keep up with exercising on a regular schedule. However, it is not necessary to join a health club in order to exercise! Simply walking regularly around the block, the shopping mall, or the park can provide the needed exercise.

If you have ataxia and want to begin an exercise program, first consult with your physician to find out if there are any restrictions on what you may do because of your ataxia or any other medical condition. A physical therapist may be able to provide some instructions or suggestions about exercises or a stretching program that you can do at home. If you join a class at a health club, make sure the instructor knows about your ataxia so that you can select the right class for your abilities.

The National Ataxia Foundation offers the following information sheet: *Frenkel's Exercises for Ataxic Conditions.* See the Resources section at the back of this book for contact information.

Getting proper
NUTRITION
and concerns with eating and choking

A NUTRITIOUS DIET is important for everyone, but it is especially vital for people who are disabled, whose ability to exercise is limited, or who may be susceptible to infections. Not only that, eating is one of the great pleasures of life, so the challenge and pleasure comes in finding foods that are nutritious, easy to eat *and* tasty.

Basic nutrition information is available from your State Department of Public Health, the public library, or from a dietitian or nutritionist. Consult your physician or a trained nutritionist before making significant changes in diet. (Your doctor can help you find a dietitian or nutritionist.)

Nutrition do's:

- Eat at least three meals a day.
- Start the day with a breakfast that includes adequate protein to get you energized for the day.

- Eat adequate amounts of the basic food groups each day: vegetables/fruits, whole grains/ cereals, nuts/legumes, dairy products/meats.
- Emphasize fresh and natural

foods, since they are generally more nutritious than canned, frozen or preserved. Prolonged cooking of fruits and vegetables leads to a significant loss of vitamins.

- Choose lighter meats, such as poultry, fish, and lamb, over red meats. (In general, Americans eat more red meats than necessary.) It's also possible to obtain sufficient protein by eating very little meat, and a lot of whole grains, nuts, eggs, dairy products, and fish.

Nutrition don'ts:

- Don't overindulge in sweets and highly refined or rich foods. They are generally unhealthy and may increase shakiness.
- Don't make coffee a regular habit. Moderate to large amounts of coffee might make tremors or shaking worse.
- Don't drink alcoholic beverages. Most people with ataxia note that incoordination is worsened by alcohol consumption.
- Don't take mega-vitamin supplements unless they are specifically prescribed by your doctor. Overdoses of certain vitamins can cause neurologic damage. If you are avoiding certain foods because of difficulty swallowing or other reasons, vitamin or mineral supplements may be necessary, but inform your doctor of any vitamins, minerals or extracts you are taking.
- If you have difficulty swallowing during meals, don't consume mucus-forming foods such as milk, cream, ice cream and other milk products. If dairy products are eliminated from the diet, it's important to supplement with other sources of calcium, such as hard cheeses, dark green leafy vegetables and dried legumes.

When swallowing is difficult

As ataxia progresses, swallowing may become increasingly difficult. When difficulties are noted, it is important to get an assessment of the swallowing mechanism by a speech pathologist who may be able to recommend specific changes in position, eating equipment, or food preparation that will make eating a more pleasant experience. (Your physician can help you find a speech pathologist.) The speech pathologist may recommend foods that are well-cooked or pureed in a blender or food processor for easier swallowing. Meat will be easier to swallow if it is tender, moist and cut into small portions or pureed. Bones should be completely removed from chicken or fish before serving.

To make swallowing easier:
- Sit fully erect.
- Keep head erect with the chin tucked down toward the chest during swallowing.
- Take small bites, eat slowly and chew thoroughly.
- Alternate bites of solids with sips of liquids.
- Use a straw to drink liquids that are room temperature or cold.
- Concentrate while eating to help prevent choking.
- Eat in a quiet, relaxed atmosphere.

When choking is a problem

Choking is common in people whose ataxia affects their ability to speak or swallow. It is very important for the person with ataxia and his or her family to know how to minimize the risk of choking incidents and how to help when they do occur.

What you should know about coughing:

- Coughing is an important defense against choking. It can clear the airways of large particles (such as food) and tiny particles (such as bacteria). A person who is able to cough normally is better off than someone who has a weak cough or is unable to cough at all. When someone is  coughing strongly during a choking incident it is a good sign, even though it might sound and look frightening to observers. A good coughing spell during a choking incident generally means the person will be okay.

- Inability to cough due to food blocking the airway is an emergency; it means the victim can't breathe. If the obstruction is not removed, the victim will lose consciousness from lack of air and die within a matter of minutes.

Heimlich maneuver Encourage friends and family to learn the Heimlich maneuver. When a choking victim is unable to breathe or cough, you must apply the Heimlich maneuver to dislodge the particle blocking the airway. To learn this, contact your local Red Cross or nearby hospital or school to find out when they offer an emergency care course.

The Heimlich maneuver has three steps:

1) Use index finger to clear any materials within reach in the victim's mouth.

2) Deliver five sharp blows to the victim's upper back with cupped hand or fist.

3) Deliver five sharp upward thrusts to the upper abdomen with fisted hands.

Repeat steps until the obstruction is relieved.

It is important to practice the Heimlich maneuver with an instructor. Techniques used on infants or children are slightly different. On adults, the technique varies depending on whether the victim is sitting or lying down. It is also possible to injure internal organs, particularly with the abdominal thrusts, if the procedure is not performed correctly.

Managing chronic aspiration

Chronic aspiration is less dramatic but it is still a serious form of choking that is very common in people with ataxia. Chronic aspiration occurs when small amounts of food or saliva leak frequently into the airway and down into the lungs. (When the coordination of tongue, lip, jaw and swallowing movement is poor, only some of the food goes into the esophagus during swallowing. Some stays in the mouth, and some gets into the airways.)

Chronic aspiration often occurs without much choking or coughing. It usually happens to people who have a poorly coordinated swallow and a weak cough mechanism. Because small particles of food and saliva contain bacteria, chronic aspiration can lead to chronic or acute lung infections called "aspiration pneumonia."

Minimizing risks associated with chronic aspiration:

- Since certain textures of food might be more difficult than others for the person with ataxia to swallow, avoid those that tend to cause the most problems including thin liquids, dry or pasty foods, and anything with large chunks.

- Consult a speech pathologist if coughing or choking occurs frequently during meals. Ask about appropriate techniques to lower the risk of choking. Techniques might vary from person to person, but often include proper positioning of the head and body, altering the texture of the food, alternating solids and liquids and taking care to chew food slowly.

- Encourage coughing to help clear materials out of the lungs and airways.
- Remove any food particles remaining in the mouth after a meal.
- Avoid lying down right after meals, since it tends to promote lung infections. Any kind of movement will help clear aspirated materials from the lungs.
- Take good care of the mouth and teeth. Clean teeth at least daily (preferably more often), and schedule regular dental checkups. An abscessed tooth can lead to loss of appetite and weight loss, and ultimately may need to be removed. Talking and eating are more enjoyable and more natural with one's own teeth than with a dental plate or dentures.

When tube feeding is necessary

If eating becomes too tiring or difficult, or if aspiration pneumonias have occurred several times or weight loss occurs despite everyone's best attempts, it may be appropriate to consider tube feedings. Tube feedings require a tube that goes directly into the stomach or intestines, and a liquid formula that provides all the necessary nutrients.

Most often, when tube feedings are planned to continue indefinitely, a tube is inserted through the skin directly into the stomach and then sewn into place. A tube like this is called a gastrostomy tube. For most people, a gastrostomy tube can be placed using sedation and local anesthetic. General anesthesia is usually not necessary. Once in place, gastrostomy tubes do not cause pain or discomfort.

Complications of gastrostomy tubes can include the tube falling out, irritation of the skin around the tube, infection, or leakage of gastric juices around the tube.

Nutrition provided through a gastrostomy tube can include any fluid. Usually, to meet all of the individual's nutritional needs, high quality, carefully formulated solutions containing vitamins, minerals and high protein content are used. These include formulas such as Ensure and Resource, among others. A nutritionist can help the family and physician to select the correct amounts of the correct formula, based on the individual's weight, body size and health status.

Although gastrostomy tube feedings can solve the problem of getting enough calories into a person with ataxia, a gastrostomy tube does not prevent a person from choking on or aspirating saliva. And some physicians think that the risk of heartburn (or "reflux esophagitis") is higher in people who have a gastrostomy tube. For many people, the decision whether or when to use a gastrostomy tube is not an easy one. Fortunately, it is not usually an emergency, so you have time to talk with your doctor, other professionals, friends and family about the issues and to make the decision that is best for you.

SPEAKING problems and helps

SPEECH IS usually affected by ataxia. Slurring of words (dysarthria) is caused by reduced coordination, slowness, and inaccuracy of movement of the tongue, lips, and jaw.

Dysarthric speech

Characteristics of dysarthric speech:
- imprecise consonant production
- excess and equal stress on syllables
- prolonged or shortened sounds
- slow rate
- harsh voice
- lack of loudness variation
- monotone pitch

Speech evaluation and counseling is a valuable aid to help you deal with speech difficulty. For help with your speech and communication, contact a speech pathologist in your area. Speech pathologists may be located through physician referral, hospitals, rehabilitation centers, schools and universities, and speech and hearing clinics.

Contact the American Speech and Hearing Association at 10801 Rockville Pike, Rockville, MD 20852 or contact your state speech and hearing association.

Suggestions for maintaining speech clarity:

- Do not try to talk as rapidly as you did before. Concentrate on a slower speaking pace.
- Attempt to exaggerate the movements of your tongue, lips, and jaw while talking.
- Divide your sentences into phrases. Take more pauses for breathing.
- Pronounce long words by dividing them into syllables, saying each separately, as: *in-tell-i-gent.*
- Practice the above steps in front of a mirror. Read word lists and newspapers before you use this control with your family and others.
- If possible, tape record some of these sessions and play them back to hear where you need practice.
- Explaining your problem can put others at ease.

 Tell your listeners that you are trying to make your speech more understandable. Ask them to be patient.

- If you cannot adequately express yourself orally, there are alternate means of communication. With a word board, you point to words to communicate. Another way is to use a portable electronic device activated by switches to indicate your communication needs.

Note: *Hereditary Ataxia: A Guidebook for Managing Speech and Swallowing Problems* ($3.50, shipping included) is available from the National Ataxia Foundation. Written in 1982, but still helpful. See the Resources section of this book for the address.

JOB ISSUES to consider

THE DISABILITIES that invariably accompany ataxia and other neurological diseases are bound to create challenges in finding and retaining employment. However, many people with ataxia find meaningful employment for many years.

Earl McLaughlin, of California, was diagnosed with ataxia at age 21, but that didn't stop him from going to college and attaining full-time employment as an accountant. At 38, he continues to work full-time and is happy with his job at the utility company where he has worked for more than 12 years.

Earl's advice to others with ataxia is to "be positive." He also recommends getting as much education as possible. Earl admits that having ataxia might require patience and persistence in seeking a job: "Since I had a high grade point average, my resume looked good and it was easy to land first interviews. I don't like to make excuses, but my speech was affected when I would get nervous and I suspect that influenced my chances of getting called back for second interviews. I just kept trying. I was always very open about the fact that I have ataxia, but I'd also point out that I was a hard worker. I feel that everything turned out for the best."

The degree of difficulty you experience in obtaining employment will depend on many factors, including your age, education, aptitude and physical capabilities.

Factors to consider when seeking a job

- What types of work am I capable of doing given my current physical limitations?
- How long am I likely to be able to continue functioning at my present level?
- What types of jobs have a future in the labor market?
- What kind of training does the job require?
- Which educational institutions provide the training I would need, and how accessible are they?
- Is there financial aid available for any training required?

Discussing your needs with your employer

Although some people with ataxia say they hesitate to discuss their condition with their employer for fear of losing their jobs, in many cases doing so helps clear up misunderstandings and opens the door for exploration of options that work best for both employer and employee.

For instance, a Minnesota man with ataxia reports that he was suspected of having a drinking problem until he explained the cause of his unsteady gait. Once he did so, much tension was relieved and his employer arranged his work schedule in a manner that required less mobility.

Before talking to your employer about job accommodations, think through your approach. Start by focusing on the positive. Emphasize your capabilities and what you can continue to offer the company. Explain how any adjustments made will help you perform your job more effectively.

Altering your work schedule or environment

Work options might include:

- switching from full time to part time
- scheduling frequent rest breaks to restore energy
- designing a flexible schedule that allows you to work during times your energy level is highest or during times when getting to and from work is least stressful
- modifying your work area to enable you to work more comfortably and efficiently

If you become physically incapable of handling the responsibilities of your current job, talk to your employer about possibilities for lighter assignments within the organization before seeking employment elsewhere. This will provide the opportunity for continuity of any benefits you are currently receiving from the company.

Employers vary in their responses to special requests from employees. Some will go out of their way to accommodate the needs of an employee, while others are not as responsive.

In 1990, the Americans with Disabilities Act (ADA) was passed, requiring employers to make adjustments and accommodations for people with disabilities. As of July 1994, companies with 15 or more employees are required to follow ADA guidelines, while those with fewer than 15 employees are exempt.

Resources at larger work sites for those with disabilities might include occupational health and human resource departments. Some organizations provide ergonomic or occupational health experts to evaluate the work site to fit employees' needs. If your employer does not provide this service, you can check the telephone business directory under occupational therapy or ergonomics, or call your local hospital's occupational therapy department.

Safety considerations

Your safety and the safety of your co-workers is another factor to consider. Be realistic. If your balance is bad, and your job involves climbing ladders or walking girders, it doesn't make sense to put yourself or others in danger by attempting to retain that particular job. On other hand, don't be hasty to quit working altogether before investigating all the possibilities within your capabilities.

For many, the financial independence that a job offers contributes to self-esteem and provides a reassuring sense of structure to their daily schedule. Taking the step from employment to non-employment is a big adjustment for people with ataxia and for their families—one that should be carefully considered.

Other employment options

Besides conventional employment outside the home, consider other options. For instance, self-employment generally allows more flexibility in your work schedule, and it can often be arranged so your clients bring work to you, saving you transportation hassles to and from a work site. Bookkeeping, word processing, and childcare are a few examples of self-owned business possibilities.

Think about what you like to do. Consider expanding a hobby or interest into a money-making endeavor. Do you like photography, arts and crafts, or writing? Do you have computer skills? Abilities such as these might be turned into entrepreneurial endeavors in addition to providing personal satisfaction.

If you decide to explore "work at home" ads in the employment section of local newspapers, make a careful check of the legitimacy of any such employment offers before investing your time. Opportunities are usually available for telephone solicitors, envelope stuffers and other tasks.

If employment is unrealistic for you, you might still get satisfaction from using your skills in a volunteer capacity. After high school, Denise worked for several years in sales and purchasing for a construction equipment supplier. When fatigue became a problem, she gave up her job and now serves as a chapter leader for the National Ataxia Foundation. "I enjoyed being employed for income, but I also enjoy volunteer work, and can adjust my schedule as needed," she says.

Denise's advice to career-minded people who have ataxia is "go for it," but to focus on jobs with flexible hours and minimal mobility requirements.

Job counseling and retraining

Most large cities have programs and resources to assist people in finding employment. These programs often offer skills and interests assessment, networking, job placement assistance, retraining options and counseling. Contact the Department of Jobs and Training and the Department of Vocational Service in your area for local contacts.

The Department of Vocational Service, a federally funded organization, has offices in most major cities, and provides testing to determine your ability to perform various jobs and can direct you to local retraining resources.

Employer disability benefits

Check into short-term and long-term disability insurance benefits offered by your employer. It will be in your best interests to take advantage of insurance subsidized by your employer.

When you are no longer able to work

If you want to work, do not hesitate to explore all possible pathways back into the work place. However, if you are unable to work, avail yourself of federal and state or local resources specifically developed to assist disabled individuals.

Talk over your decision to quit work with your family and physician. When applying for Social Security Disability, it will be the responsiblity of you and your physician to explain why you are unable to work. The decisions regarding eligibility for Social Security Disability benefits are made by lawyers and judges rather than physicians. An official book lists approved diseases judged to cause disabling symptoms and serves as one guide in deciding who is eligible for disability. You might have to be persistent. About 60 percent of all disability claims are rejected initially, and claims are often only accepted after the third or fourth appeal.

Employment-related resources

Free information services:

- **The Job Accommodation Network (JAN)**
918 Chestnut Ridge Road, Suite 1
West Virginia University, P.O. Box 6080
Morgantown, WV 26506-6080
1-800-526-7234

An international toll-free consulting service that provides information about job accommodation and the employability of people with disabilities.

- **The ADA-WORK information Service**
  1-800-ADA-WORK (1-800-232-9675)

    A free information calling line. Professional consultants are available to discuss requirements of barrier-free access and other issues, employment policies, manufactured products. (Also, call this number for current information about other service agencies, training programs and funding sources.)

- **Americans with Disabilities Act (ADA)**
  For information contact:
  US Equal Opportunity Commission
  1-800-669-4000
  TTY/TTD: 800-669-6820

- **Department of Social Services** (or Office of Vocational Rehabilitation) in your state can often provide counseling. To locate, call the local Department of Social Services or welfare department.

- **Home Operated Business Opportunities for the Disabled**. From Accent Special Publications, P.O. Box 700, Bloomington, IL 61701. Cost: $4.50

Agencies:

- **Rehabilitation Services Administration**
  Division of Developmental Disabilities
  330 C Street
  Washington, DC 20201

- **The President's Committee On Employment of the Handicapped**
  Vanguard Building, Room 636
  1111 20th St. N.W.
  Washington, DC 20210

- **Association of Rehabilitation Facilities**
  5530 Wisconsin Ave., Suite 955
  Washington, DC 20015

- **Department of Human Resources** or **State Department of Rehabilitation** offer skills testing, counseling or training or education.

FINANCIAL PLANNING for a better quality of life

PLANNING YOUR financial future early in life is always wise, but it is imperative if you or your child have been diagnosed with a degenerative form of ataxia, or if you know you or your child are at risk for having ataxia. The decisions made today can greatly impact future quality of life for the person with ataxia. As ataxia progresses, there will be special needs that can't be met without adequate finances.

Government programs

A major cornerstone for your financial and estate plan could be the benefits provided by the government. Following is a brief description of the major programs. Contact your local Department of Human Services and Social Security office for details.

- **Supplemental Security Insurance (SSI)** Makes monthly payments (called Supplemental Security Income) to people with disabilities who meet the asset and income requirements. The benefit amount and eligibility information are available from your Social Security office. SSI is also available when you don't have sufficient work credits to qualify for full Social Security benefits. SSI is usually provided in conjunction with Medicaid.

- **Medicaid** A health care program for people with low income and limited assets. Medicaid is frequently available in conjunction with SSI. Medic-aid is administered by state welfare or social services agencies.

- **Medicare**   Our country's basic health insurance program for people age 65 and older. This benefit is also available to people with disabilities when they have qualified for Social Security Disability Insurance income for two years.

- **Social Security Disability Insurance (SSDI)**   Pays a benefit (called Social Security Disability Income) to people with a disability that is expected to last more than a year. The benefit begins after a six-month waiting period and is based on earned work credits. Additional benefits may be available for dependent children and a spouse. Contact your Social Security office for your benefit estimate and additional information.

When you are at risk for ataxia

If you are "at risk" for ataxia, but have not yet been diagnosed, it will be in your best interests to purchase adequate health and life insurance before any signs of the disorder are apparent. Once you have a diagnosis, purchasing or changing policies will be difficult and might even be impossible.

Disability insurance   It's best to have individual coverage, or plan to convert your group coverage when you discontinue working.

Health insurance   Make sure that your major medical coverage is "unlimited," since "limited" coverage can be terminated once the insurer has reimbursed a designated dollar amount toward your medical expenses. Consider conversion of your health coverage when you leave work. The cost can be prohibitive. Remember that you may be eligible for Medicare or Medicaid.

Life insurance   Compare the advantages of various plans. You can purchase either *term* or *cash value* policies. Term insurance costs less initially, but has no cash value, and the premiums increase on a regular schedule based on the age range of the insured person. Cash value insurance premiums cost more, but the premiums do not increase over time and they do have a cash value.

Those who are at high risk for disability are wise to consider purchasing as much term insurance as possible at the lower rate, since they will get about five times as much insurance for the dollars they spend per year over cash value insurance.

When purchasing life insurance, request the *disability waiver* rider. This rider provides that if you are disabled for six months (sometimes four months) or longer, all future premium payments are waived as long as you are disabled. The basic protection remains the same.

When your child has ataxia

Friedreich's ataxia is most often diagnosed in individuals between 10 and 18 years old. If you are the parent of a child who has been diagnosed with this or any other disabling disorder, you'll want to give early consideration to estate planning and vocational goals.

Estate planning   When your son or daughter has ataxia, strategic estate planning is important to guarantee that your child will be able to maintain the same quality of life whether you are here or not.

Young people with Friedreich's ataxia frequently haven't worked enough quarters to qualify for Medicare and SSDI. Therefore, they are much more likely to qualify for Medicaid and SSI. And since this program is not awarded to those who have more than $2,000 in assets, careful estate planning, which usually involves setting up a *supplemental needs trust* (see next paragraph), is necessary to preserve your estate while maximizing governmental benefits available for your child.

Supplemental needs trust   The supplemental needs trust (sometimes referred to as a *special needs trust*) is a fund usually established by parents to assure that their family member with a disability will always have an excellent quality of life even if the parents are no longer living.

The trust is intended to pay for those "extra" items that are not provided by or paid for by publicly funded (government) programs.

If the trust is carefully drafted, funded, and administered according to the law, the trust *won't* disqualify the beneficiary from any publicly funded programs. An example would be that to qualify for Supplemental Security Income (SSI) and Medicaid, an individual must have limited assets. The assets in a supplemental needs trust are *not* considered in calculating the eligibility for these government programs.

This trust must be carefully and properly drafted to comply with current state and federal laws and should only be attempted by an attorney with extensive experience in this area of law.

When choosing an attorney to draft your documents, ask how many supplemental needs trusts he or she has developed in the past year. If the response is less than 10, you may want to continue searching for an attorney.

Education planning—thinking ahead   While you are planning for your child's more distant needs through strategic estate planning, you can also encourage your preteen or teen with ataxia to consider career options that will enable him or her to earn an income in spite of the disabilities that will be encountered as the disease progresses. Fortunately, ataxia does not impair the mind, which improves the feasibility of maintaining jobs that require more mental rather than physical stamina.

When you are an adult with ataxia

As an adult with ataxia, your approach to financial planning will vary depending on whether you are currently employed or on disability:

Unemployed adults   If you are currently disabled and not working, it's important that you protect your family assets so they won't be used entirely for health care. Also, investigate the possibility of having any potential inheritances put in a supplemental needs trust (described on previous page) to ensure that you remain qualified for available governmental assistance in the future.

Employed adults
- Check into the conversion privileges of your group health and life insurance policies to be sure you may continue them on an individual basis after you terminate employment.
- Review the terms of any retirement/disability plan provided by your employer.
- Design your estate plan to protect the balance of your family estate when you find it necessary to quit working.
- Apply for Social Security Disability Insurance (SSDI) if you cannot adequately supplement your income by other means (such as self-employment)

once it becomes necessary for you to terminate employment. The two major benefits of SSDI are monthly income after the initial six-month waiting period, and Medicare benefits after a two-year qualifying period. To apply for SSDI, contact your nearest Social Security Office. You must have a letter from your physician stating that you are incapable of further employment for at least one year or more.

When Social Security Disability is denied   People are frequently denied Social Security Disability benefits simply because their physician did not give enough details. When applying for Social Security Disability, it's important to *be graphic.* Encourage your physician to provide more than medical terms and clinical findings. Make it clear how the symptoms affect your ability to perform your present job. Social Security will deny the claim if they feel the applicant can do *any* other job. They prefer retraining. You must have total disability to qualify. Since many Social Security employees have little or no knowledge of the ataxias, it's essential to *describe everything!* For instance, rather than simply saying the afflicted person can't walk, it's important to describe what happens when the attempt is made to do so.

Additional considerations for homeowners   If you own your home, consider mortgage insurance that includes a provision stating that in the event that the homeowner becomes disabled or dies, the insurance company will pay the mortgage in full. In any case, insurance can provide a low cost protection plan for you. Contact a local insurance agent. Before making a decision, compare the benefits of various policies to determine which will work best for you.

Resources for financial planning

Community services Check with your local Information and Referral Agency for additional services and benefits that your community may offer. These kinds of services are usually listed in the telephone business directory under the heading "Social Services." Local community services often include transportation for people with disabilities

Financial counselors, such as your banker, can provide further information on how to effectively trim your budget. Ask for ideas to help stretch your income to meet your financial needs.

Free medical care and supplies The Muscular Dystrophy Association (MDA) offers many valuable services to people with Friedreich's ataxia or Charcot-Marie-Tooth disorder, among others. In addition to free clinics for medical care, MDA provides for the purchase and repair of walkers, canes, crutches, braces, wheelchairs, orthopedic shoes, hospital beds, other medical appliances, and special aids for daily living. These items need to have been prescribed by a physician. The Association also offers other free services such as transportation to their clinics, physical therapy, if authorized, and flu inoculations. For further information or the location of your nearest MDA chapter, contact: Muscular Dystrophy Association, 3300 E. Sunrise Dr., Tucson, AZ 85718 (tel. 520-529-2000).

Life Planning for Persons with Disabilities is a Minnesota-based company that helps individuals with disabilities and their families plan their financial futures. This organization can provide consultations regarding wills, supplemental needs trust and estate planning. There is no initial consultation fee. Call 800-487-5310.

Social Security Office   To locate your nearest Social Security Office, write: U.S. Social Security Administration, Division of Disability Operations, 6401 Security Boulevard, Baltimore, MD 21235; or call 1-800-772-1213.

National Ataxia Foundation   This organization publishes a national newsletter and provides literature and other services for people with ataxia and their families. For information, contact:

National Ataxia Foundation
15500 Wayzata Boulevard, #750
Wayzata, Minnesota 55391

Telephone: 612-473-7666

Fax: 612-473-9289

E-mail: naf@mr.net

Internet home page: www.ataxia.org

Having FUN!—making leisure and recreation part of your life

I was brought up with the belief that I should just do the best I can with what I have, and have learned to focus on the positive. Having ataxia doesn't prevent me from having fun. I love meeting new people, and have found that when I initiate conversations, people soon realize that I'm just a regular person. —Denise

DENISE HAS ataxia. She leads an active social life, loves art and music, and has enjoyed traveling to such places as Europe, Canada, and Hawaii. In her travels, she finds that being in a wheelchair often provides an advantage in meeting new people. She finds that when people see her struggling to get through a door, they are likely to offer a hand, which she says makes them feel good and provides "a wonderful opportunity to strike up interesting conversations."

Leisure time activities can be a worthwhile and enjoyable part of everyone's life, regardless of disability. Recreation adds balance to life. And it often provides opportunities to meet new friends who share similar interests.

Leisure activity suggestions

Having fun doesn't necessarily mean spending a lot of money or making elaborate plans. Something as simple as thoughtfully observing the world around us can give us a renewed appreciation for life. You might be inspired to write down your observations, or capture them in drawings or in paint. It isn't necessary to try to impress others with the results. Just enjoy the process. Writing, drawing, and painting are a great way to increase observation skills.

Many kinds of games can be enjoyed by people in all stages of ataxia. Games are a great way to socialize.

If you have access to a computer, explore the Internet. You will find information on nearly every subject that interests you, and you will be able to communicate online with people around the world. See the Internet entry in the Resources section at the end of this book for more information.

Many of your favorite activities can still be pursued, perhaps in a modified way, or with the help and company of another person.

Increasingly, state and national parks and campgrounds are being made accessible. Or you might look into local facilities by calling your county or city department of parks and recreation.

Certain sports activities can still be enjoyed by people in the early stages of ataxia. Walking or hiking, bicycling, and swimming are some possibilities. A walking stick or cane can provide reassuring stability if needed. Adult tricycles are popular among people with balance problems. The three-wheeled bikes usually have roomy baskets for carrying things. In swimming pools, flotation bars provide excellent means of keeping you afloat while performing water exercises. They are available at swimming pool supply stores. Make a practice of brainstorming on your own and with others to come up with ways to adapt activities to your abilities.

Spectator sports, concerts, plays, and movies are generally accessible. Don't forget restaurants. These can all be good opportunities enjoy the company of friends and family.

The National Ataxia Foundation's chapters, support groups, "Pen Pals" program, and computer bulletin board provide opportunities for individuals and families affected by ataxia to make new friends and learn from one another. See Resources section for information.

Adult education or college courses can be taken for fun or to learn new skills. Community education programs offer informal (no grading!) classes on hobby skills and practical topics such as small-business accounting.

Consult your local public librarian for books, magazines, brochures, etc., on accessible recreation opportunities. (The library can be a useful source of information on all aspects of having a disability.)

Remember that you are still a part of your community even if you have ataxia. Don't stagnate. Try to avoid the pitfall of staying home or only going out with the family. Try not to be self-conscious. Uninformed people may be curious, but most people are genuinely interested in others. Give people the chance to learn. They may even want to help if they can. People need you to teach them these things. Yes, some people are curious—but equally true, there are compassionate people who choose to be part of your world, who choose to be your friend.

Glossary

abetalipoproteinemia—One of several metabolic diseases that can cause progressive ataxia.

acetazolamide—Diuretic sometimes used to treat muscle twitchings and nystagmus associated with EA2.

alpha-fetoprotein (AFP)—A protein formed in the liver of a fetus. Normally, small amounts are present in the amniotic fluid and in the mother's blood. AFP levels are usually high in people who have ataxia telangectasia.

argininosuccinic aciduria—One of several metabolic disorders that can result in episodes of ataxia (poor coordination).

ataxia—Poor coordination. Can be used to refer to a neurologic symptom which can have many causes or to denote one of several degenerative diseases that cause poor coordination.

autosomal dominant ataxia—A disorder in which the ataxia-causing gene is located on an autosome and in which only one ataxia-causing gene needs to be inherited for symptoms to be expressed.

autosomal recessive ataxia—A disorder or disease in which the ataxia-causing gene is located on an autosome and for which inheritance of two copies of the ataxia-causing gene must have been inherited for symptoms to be expressed.

autosome—Any chromosome that is not a sex chromosome. Autosomes come in pairs (one member of each pair from each parent) so that each gene on an autosome is present in two copies.

Behr's syndrome—One of several degenerative disorders of unknown cause which often include ataxia as a prominent symptom.

biotinidase deficiency—One of several metabolic disorders that can result in episodes of ataxia (poor coordination).

central nervous system—The brain and spinal cord.

cerebellum—The coordination center of the brain, located at the back of the brain.

cerebellar degeneration—Degeneration of the cerebellum, which is the coordination center of the brain. Can be caused by a number of hereditary or non-hereditary conditions.

ceroid lipofuscinosis—One of several degenerative metabolic disorders of unknown cause in which progressive ataxia can be a prominent symptom.

chorea—Jerky involuntary body movements.

chromosomes—Spaghetti-like structures (visible only through a microscope) that contain the genetic material (DNA) that determines hereditary characteristics. Each cell in the human body contains 23 pairs of chromosomes, 22 of which are called autosomes. The 23rd pair are referred to as sex chromosomes and determine the sex of the individual.

cognitive—Having to do with the ability to think or the manner in which one thinks.

computerized tomography (CT)—A sophisticated x-ray technique that visualizes sections of the body with a special scanner. Also sometimes referred to as computerized axial tomography (CAT)

contractures—Tightening of tendons that results in shrinkage or shortening of a muscle.

CT (or CAT)—See computerized tomography.

degenerative—Characterized by deterioration and loss of function.

dementia—A disorder of mental processes that can include memory problems, personality changes, impaired reasoning and disorientation. May have many different causes.

dysarthric speech (dysarthria)—Speech in which pronunciation is unclear. May be mild or severe.

dystonia—Disorder caused by prolonged muscle spasms that hold part of the body in an unnatural posture or cause twisting and repetitive movements .

dentato-rubro-pallido-luysian atrophy (DRPLA)—Rare hereditary form of adult-onset ataxia named after the parts of the brain most affected by the disease.

DRPLA—See dentato-rubro-pallido-luysian atrophy.

EA1 and EA2—See episodic ataxia.

EKG—See electrocardiogram.

electrocardiogram (EKG or ECG)—Medical test that records electrical activity of the heart.

electromyography (EMG)—Test that records the electrical activity of a muscle by means of electrodes inserted into muscles. Often combined with a nerve conduction velocity (NCV) test.

EMG—See electromyography.

epilepsy—Disorder of brain function that results in recurrent seizures. Can have many possible causes.

episodic ataxias (EA1 and EA2)—Autosomal dominant forms of hereditary ataxia that usually begin in the teenage years and involve episodes of ataxia and dysarthria (impaired speech) often brought on by exercise.

Friedreich's ataxia—Recessive form of hereditary ataxia that affects the nerve pathways in the spinal cord and typically begins in childhood or teen years. Most common form of early-onset ataxia.

gene—A unit of instruction for producing a specific body protein. Each gene has a particular location on a specific chromosome. Humans have about 100,000 genes, each duplicated in every body cell. When a gene does not work properly, the protein it codes for may be made improperly or not at all, which can cause the symptoms of a genetic disease.

genetic—Having to do with genes.

Gillespie's syndrome—A form of ataxia caused by faulty formation of the cerebellum during development before birth.

granule cell hypoplasia—A form of ataxia caused by faulty formation of the cerebellum during development before birth.

Hartnup disease—One of several metabolic disorders that can result in episodes of ataxia (poor coordination).

hereditary olivopontocerebellar atrophy (OPCA)—See spinocerebellar ataxia type 1.

Holmes ataxia—See spinocerebellar ataxia type 5.

hyperornithinemia—One of several metabolic disorders that can result in episodes of ataxia (poor coordination).

hypogonadism—Underdevelopment of reproductive system. May occur with ataxia in several very rare disorders, such as Richards-Rundle syndrome.

immunoglobulins—Body proteins that serve as antibodies. The human body manufactures five types of immunoglobulins, each having a different function.

intention tremor—A tremor that occurs when the afflicted individual tries to reach for or touch an object.

isovaleric acidemia—One of several metabolic disorders that can result in episodes of ataxia (poor coordination).

Joubert's syndrome—One of several forms of ataxia caused by faulty formation of the cerebellum during development before birth.

Leigh's syndrome—One of several metabolic disorders that can result in episodes of ataxia (poor coordination).

leukodystrophies—One of several metabolic diseases that can cause progressive ataxia.

Lincoln's ataxia (or Lincoln's disease)—See spinocerebellar ataxia type 5.

magnetic resonance imaging (MRI)—A technique that relies on magnetic fields to produce computerized pictures of soft tissues of the body. Allows viewing of delicate nerve fibers in the spinal cord and differentiates types of brain tissue.

Machado-Joseph disease (MJD)—An autosomal dominant form of hereditary ataxia that usually begins in mid-adult life. Also sometimes called SCA3.

Marie's ataxia—See spinocerebellar ataxia type 1.

Marinesco-Sjögrens syndrome—One of several degenerative disorders of unknown origin in which ataxia is often a prominent symptom.

metabolic disorder—Disease caused by enzyme deficiencies. Most are autosomal recessive.

mitochondrial encephalomyopathies—Metabolic diseases that can cause progressive ataxia. The mitochondria are the "energy storehouses" of the cell. Ataxia and the other neurologic symptoms are common in almost all mitochondrial diseases.

MJD—See Machado-Joseph disease.

MRI—See magnetic resonance imaging.

multiple carboxylase deficiency—One of several metabolic disorders that can result in episodes of ataxia (poor coordination).

mutation—A variation or mistake in a gene that is significant enough to cause disease.

myoclonic seizures—Sudden spasmodic seizures that result in jerking or flexing movements.

myoclonus—Sudden spasms of muscles.

NCV test (nerve conduction velocity test)—Relies on small electrical impulses to measure the speed at which nerves are transmitting messages. (Test is administered by placing electrodes on the skin.)

neurologic disorders—Disorders involving the nervous system.

neuropathy—See peripheral neuropathy.

nystagmus—Rapid involuntary movements of the eye that may be side to side, up and down or circling.

oculomotor apraxia—An eye disorder that involves difficulty in moving the eyes from side to side without also moving the head.

optic atrophy—Sporadic olivopontocerebellar ataxia

ornithine transcarbamylase deficiency—One of several metabolic disorders that can result in episodes of ataxia (poor coordination).

peripheral nervous system—The part of the nervous system lying outside the brain and spinal cord including the motor and sensory nerves in the arms and legs.

peripheral nerves—Nerves that make up the peripheral nervous system, including the cranial nerves, and the nerves that leave the spinal cord to pass information between the brain and the body and limbs.

peripheral neuropathy—Dysfunction of the peripheral nerves, usually affecting the largest nerves first. May have many hereditary or non-hereditary causes. Usually causes weakness or loss of sensation of the feet, legs or hands.

pes cavus—Excessively high arched feet causing an unnaturally high instep. Also known as clawfoot.

polymorphism—A variation or mistake in the structure of a gene that does not result in harmful effects.

pyruvate dehydrogenase deficiency—One of several metabolic disorders that can result in episodes of ataxia (poor coordination).

recessive gene—A gene whose effect will only appear in individuals when its partner gene (or allele) is the same type. (For instance a gene pair might include one allele that codes for brown eyes and one allele that codes for blue eyes. Since the gene for blue eyes is recessive, the individual will have brown eyes. The individual will only have blue eyes if both of the paired genes (alleles) code for blue eyes.

retinitis pigmentosa—Degeneration of the retina, with clumps of pigment visible when the retina is examined. May have several different causes, and can rarely be seen in association with ataxia or cerebellar degeneration.

retinopathy—Any disorder of the retina involving impairment or loss of vision. (The retina is a light-sensitive layer that lines the interior of the eye.)

rigidity—Stiffening of body limbs causing resistance to passive movement. May be seen with and difficult to distinguish from spasticity.

scoliosis—Lateral (sideways) curvature of the spine.

spasticity—Condition that causes resistance of a limb to passive movements, but that allows the limb to give way when increased pressure is applied.

SCA1—See spinocerebellar ataxia type 1.

SCA2—See spinocerebellar ataxia type 2.

SCA3—See Machado-Joseph disease.

SCA4—See spinocerebellar ataxia type 4.

SCA5—See spinocerebellar ataxia type 5.

SCA7—See spinocerebellar ataxia type 7.

Schut's disease—See spinocerebellar ataxia type 1.

spinocerebellar ataxia type 1 (SCA1)—An autosomal dominant form of the disease ataxia that is hereditary and usually starts in adulthood. Also called Schut's disease, hereditary olivopontocerebellar atrophy (OPCA), or Marie's ataxia.

spinocerebellar ataxia type 2 (SCA2)—An autosomal dominant adult-onset form of ataxia that is hereditary and often causes very slow eye movements in addition to ataxia.

spinocerebellar ataxia type 4 (SCA4)—An autosomal dominant form of ataxia that is hereditary and usually starts in adulthood.

spinocerebellar ataxia type 5 (SCA5)—An autosomal dominant form of ataxia that usually starts in adulthood and is more limited to the cerebellum than other dominant ataxias. Also known as Holmes ataxia.

spinocerebellar ataxia type 7 (SCA7)—An autosomal dominant form of ataxia that is hereditary and usually starts with changes in vision acuity and color vision. Also called autosomal dominant cerebellar ataxia type 2 or ataxia with pigmentary retinopathy.

sporadic ataxia—A form of the disease ataxia in which symptoms begin in adulthood in an individual having no known family members with the disease.

sporadic olivopontocerebellar ataxia (or sporadic OPCA)—A form of sporadic ataxia with symptoms, in addition to ataxia, such as neuropathy, dementia, weakness, rigidity or spasticity of the muscles.

structural ataxia—Ataxia caused by improper development of the cerebellum.

Tay-Sach's disease—One of several metabolic diseases that can cause progressive ataxia.

telangiectasia—An abnormal tangle of capillary blood vessels.

tremor—Rhythmical alternating movement of a body part.

Vitamin E deficiency—Rare but treatable cause of ataxia.

Wilson's disease—One of several metabolic diseases that can cause progressive ataxia.

Resources

National Ataxia Foundation (NAF)   Everyone needs help at times, and we all can give it, too. The National Ataxia Foundation encourages you to consider its chapters and support groups as extended family where members help each other. Group members can assist people affected by ataxia who need help in going shopping, to movies or parks, and other activities. If you would like help, see if someone in your support group would enjoy doing these things with you. If you do not have an NAF chapter or support group in your area, the national office will be able to offer suggestions and assist you in starting one. Contact the national office of the NAF at :

> National Ataxia Foundation
> 15500 Wayzata Boulevard, #750
> Wayzata, Minnesota 55391
> *Telephone:* (612)473-7666
> *Fax:* (612)473-9289
> *E-mail:* naf@mr.net
> *Internet home page:* www.ataxia.org

Resources available from the National Ataxia Foundation

Fact sheets/brochures from NAF:

Ataxia—Describes ataxia as a symptom (lack of coordination) and its association with other medical problems as well as the hereditary types.

Ataxia Telangiectasia—Defines AT, its symptoms, associated potential complications, genetic pattern, etc.

Essential Tremor—Published by National Institutes of Health. Describes this hereditary neurological disorder.

Financial Planning—Lists potential resources and discusses general financial concerns.

Frenkel's Exercises for Ataxic Conditions—Exercise program for those with ataxia (with physician approval).

Friedreich's Ataxia (FA)—Describes symptoms, diagnosis, genetics. Hints on coping.

Gary Morris (fact sheet)—Tells about NAF's national spokesperson's involvement with NAF and personal experience with ataxia.

Gene Testing for Ataxia—Who should consider gene testing, what the testing can accomplish, where the testing can be done.

Health Care Coverage for Ataxia Patients—Information about health insurance policies and government assistance.

Hereditary Ataxia (brochure)—General information about the dominant and recessive ataxias, and about the National Ataxia Foundation.

Hereditary Ataxia: The Facts—Briefly describes the characteristics of recessive and dominant forms of hereditary ataxias. Defines goals of National Ataxia Foundation. (Ideal for mass distribution.)

Hereditary Olivopontocerebellar Atrophy (OPCA)—Describes genetics, symptoms, and testing for this dominantly inherited type of ataxia. Lists other commonly used names of the disease.

NAF Ambassador Program—Describes how individuals can help the National Ataxia Foundation by becoming an NAF community ambassador. Includes application form.

Pen Pal Membership—Information on joining National Ataxia Foundation's Pen Pals, which offers an opportunity to correspond with others in a similar situation.

Pen Pal Directory—NAF Pen Pals by state (nationally) and by country (internationally). Available only to Pen Pal members.

Regional Neurological Resources—Regional (USA only) lists of neurologists specializing in ataxia diagnosis and management.

Spastic Paraplegia—Defines the condition; symptoms, inheritance patterns, testing, etc.

Sporadic Olivopontocerebellar Atrophy—Describes the form of OPCA with no known family history. Symptoms and diagnostic procedure.

Students with Friedreich's Ataxia—Information for parents, teachers, and others who need to understand the physical limitations of students with FA in the classroom.

Other books/booklets from NAF:

Hereditary Ataxia: A Guidebook for Managing Speech and Swallowing Problems—Written in 1982 but still helpful. Describes problems, offers exercises and other suggestions. Available from NAF for $3.50 (includes shipping).

Living with Ataxia: An Information and Resource Guide—More than 100 pages of practical information and resources for individuals and families affected by ataxia.

Ten Years to Live, by Henry Schut—The story of the Schut family's struggle with hereditary ataxia and the impact it had on this large extended family. 1990 edition. Paperback. Includes photos. Available from NAF for $8.75 (includes shipping).

What Kids Want to Know About Ataxia—Addresses the concerns of children and teens diagnosed with ataxia. Written in a sensitive, easy-to-understand style, this 30-page booklet models a positive approach to the practical aspects of living with ataxia.

NAF quarterly newsletter:

Generations—a 40-page newsletter published three or four times per year. Includes research updates, NAF news, chapter and support group contacts and personal stories of people who live with ataxia. Single sample copies available free from NAF. National Ataxia Foundation members are added to the newsletter mailing list.

NAF ataxia video:

Together...There Is Hope—This 28-minute VHS tape discusses the ataxias, genetic patterns of inheritance, and the accomplishments and goals of the National Ataxia Foundation. Available from NAF for $20 per tape (includes shipping).

Scientific articles:

NAF provides a current comprehensive list of articles about ataxia which have been published in medical journals.

Support groups   If there isn't an NAF chapter or support group in your area, try visiting a support group for people with similar physical challenges such as head injury or multiple sclerosis. You may find it very helpful to be part of a group where you can meet other people who are experiencing the same kinds of problems, hopes, and fears as yours. These groups can serve as useful information resources. You may learn many new things about what your community has to offer to people with disabilities.

Internet   If you have even minimal computer skills and access to the Internet, you can find a world of people and information on nearly every subject. Are you interested in gardening, cooking, pets, travel, politics or a multitude of other topics? Communicate informally in chat groups with people who share your interests, or search databases for the latest technical information. Visit the home page of the National Ataxia Foundation (http://www.ataxia.org) to find information about the history and activities of NAF, a listing of NAF chapters and support groups, and links to the latest medical developments in ataxia research. Contact NAF for a brochure explaining in detail what is available through your computer.

If you are new to computers, ask a knowledgeable friend to show you what it's all about. Or you might take a beginner's class, perhaps through a community education program.

Libraries—doing your own research Public, hospital and biomedical libraries at universities offer opportunities for you to do your own research on general topics such as chronic illness, medical tests and medications, or to research specific diseases or symptoms. Looking up references and cross-referencing sources can help you find pertinent information. Before beginning your research, you might want to purchase a medical dictionary to look up definitions of unfamiliar words.

To find out what books are available on a particular topic, check the library subject file or look under subjects in *Books in Print* (published yearly by R.R. Bowker). To find articles, look at periodical subject files. If your public library does not have a particular publication you are interested in, a reference librarian might be able to obtain it through an inter-library loan.

For in-depth research, visit hospital medical libraries or biomedical libraries at universities. Photocopy machines are generally available for making copies of articles from medical journals or excerpts from medical reference books. If you would like assistance from a librarian, call ahead for an appointment so that you can visit the libraries during times when they are less heavily used by doctors, nurses, social workers, or students.

Activism   If you are activist-minded, you may wish to become involved in a group that advocates for people with disabilities. Promoting accessibility and lobbying for legislation are important activities for such groups.

General books on related topics   Following are just a few examples of books available at public and other libraries on topics pertinent to people with illness and their families. Look under various topics (such as chronic illness, disease, medical tests, doctors, patients) to find resources that might provide useful information on managing your life with ongoing medical problems.

Healing Wounded Doctor-Patient Relationships, by Linda Hanner and John J. Witek, M.D. Kashan Publishing, 1995. Tells how doctors and patients can develop healthy, productive relationships. Models how to be assertive in getting medical needs met without alienating physicians.

We Are Not Alone: Learning to Live with Chronic Illness, by Sefra Kobrin Pitzele. Workman Publishing, 1985. Covers a range of topics including getting a diagnosis, understanding the grief associated with illness, redefining relationships, and adaptive living strategies.

Mainstay: For the Well Spouse of the Chronically Ill, by Maggie Strong. Little Brown and Company, 1988. A personal story that recognizes the legitimate needs and frustrations of those who live with chronically ill spouses.

We trust that the information in this book has been useful. If you have any suggestions for future editions, please contact the National Ataxia Foundation.